Blockchain Secrets

An A-Z Guide On How To Take Your Blockchain Idea To The Market

Jag Jassel

Copyright © 2018

All Rights Reserved

ISBN: 9781731202956

Dedication

To my wife Prethika, my children Aanav and Preja, my mother Jasbir and my In-laws Sachida & Veera without whom this book have never been completed.

Acknowledgment

To my mentors, coaches and gurus, without your help, this would just be a dream!

About The Author

Jag is the Founder & CEO of **Jassel Media**.

He is in the business of building and managing brands. He is assisting businesses with strategic planning, sales and marketing to help them grow faster!

Preface

Foreword

Firstly I want to thank Jag for putting together a marvelous book and taking the time to educate us all, it is rare to find someone this dedicated to helping others, thank you brother!!

Reader, I want you to feel excited, if you are reading this book you are holding in your hands the blueprint for the biggest opportunity we will see in our lifetime.
It is very rare to be at the front of a brand new world changing technology,

This won't be a disruption it will be a complete destruction of the old way that will bring forward a complete new world - like the automobile, plane, computers and others revolutions have before this will likely be the most dramatic

We are standing on the edge of a dead forest and the match has been lit, there is no turning back from this point, what we have is about to be burnt to the ground and replaced with something new… it is exciting and scary at the same time. However what comes after a forest fire is new growth, evolution and opportunity - we have been needing this fire for a LONG TIME

The opportunity for you is massive and this is why you are reading this book, on some level you know you want to be a part of the new world, the new way and you want to ensure you and your family are not burnt to the ground but instead are part of the rebuilding team, there will be more billionaires made from this shift than anything before. I hope you are excited

This book will serve as your guide to navigate this point in time, you will come back to it and Reread it to understand what is happening, you will share it with friends and it will ensure you are ahead of the game

Listening to Jags story, he has a unique ability to pick what will happen in the future and capitalise on it, that is why this book is so important you are gaining an insight into a true entrepreneur visionary. This book will change your life, if you let it.

over my time empowering thousands through my workshops and building multiple successful companies I know there are 2 types of people who get a book like this and only one is successful. One type is the info-seeker, they read and take no action - their life never changes and the other is the info-action taker, they get the right info and then put it into action, which one are you going to be?

It is time to get committed, only 10% of people who start a book like this finish it, and even less finish it. My question to you is why are you committed to finishing this? It wont change your life sitting on the shelf!!!

Read it

Christopher M Duncan

Contents

Dedication i

Acknowledgment ii

About The Author iii

Preface iv

Introduction 1

Chapter 1. Blockchain Revolution 11

Chapter 2. Overview Of An ICO 38

Chapter 3. Vision 60

Chapter 4. Whitepaper 77

Chapter 5. Website 93

Chapter 6. Marketing 111

Chapter 7. Team 126

Chapter 8. Minimal Viable Product 142

Chapter 9. Rules & Regulations 157

Chapter 10. Crowdfunding & Pitch 171

Chapter 11. Launch 190

Page Left Blank Intentionally

Introduction

It was May 2018, a friend called me at 10PM saying, do you know that EOS ended up raising 4 Billion in their ICO funding? I was not only surprised but was gobsmacked. I couldn't believe what I was hearing. This one thing will change the fund-raising landscape of the business world in the coming years, everyone mark my words.

My love affair with technology started in the early 90s, before the Internet and iPhone. At a very young age, I discovered a real passion for working with computers. I never thought I would be working with technology whilst in university. Initially, I chose B.Com degree because a cousin had recently graduated and gained employment in a Chartered Accountancy (CA) firm. He was doing well for himself and I was told that I will make good money so I too started Commerce.

JAG JASSEL

You may have guessed by now that I was growing up in India. At that time, the technology we are using today was just a dream and learning computer skills was very awkward for many people. I decided to take a stand against the sayings of the society and started computer classes in the evenings, in addition to my regular university classes.

As long as I can remember I have always been fascinated by the business and technology world. That childish fascination has not left me but deepened over the years. During my childhood, I sold toy cars, which I had made myself using large matchboxes, LR44 batteries and a cassette tape player motor. The kids in the neighbourhood loved my battery powered cars and within a few months, I had a little enterprise going. A friend and I manufactured the toy cars and a few other friends helped to sell them in the schools nearby. It was a profitable business and we started to make $10 to $20 profit each month which was so much in those days that we didn't even know what to do with that much money!

BLOCKCHAIN SECRETS

Even at this time, I used to think about how we can use the latest technologies in toy cars to make them more attractive to the local children. We (my friends and I) spent most of our time secretly building cars in fear of our parents finding out. They were quite conservative and felt all our free time should be dedicated to studying.

A few months and lengthy board meetings later, we decided not to continue with the toy car making business, Unknowingly, I had applied principles from of The Law of Success to my first business. I was passionate, confident, imaginative, took massive action, had a team and mentors, was doing more than what I was getting paid for, and contributing in society by giving away some percentage of our profit.

After we moved on, we started making slingshots where we found a great unique value proposition. Most of the slingshots sold by the shops nearby were using leather as a firing mechanism, which had less force and wasn't durable. We replaced the leather and started using latex surgical tub which had greater force and was more durable. We had a great run for 3 months and sold many slingshots. Soon the local stores caught up and started manufacturing similar slingshots. Pity that we didn't know anything about patents otherwise we would have captured the world slingshot market by now.

Growing up, my insatiable curiosity led me to disassemble pretty much every toy I've ever had, then reassemble them in perfect working order after having carefully inspected the internal working parts. I made a habit to explore technologies being used in various products. During which time, I found new tools which helped me to improve my skills. It is a natural and golden principle that whenever one explores something, he/she will learn something new. The more I worked to understand technology the more knowledge I obtained.

Studying text books to cram never worked for me so I always did very poorly in the school and my teachers were not happy. They always said, 'You are an intelligent kid, why don't you spend more time studying rather than doing these silly things?'. I guess, studying just to get high grades wasn't very motivating and so I did the bare minimum in order to pass the grade.

I managed to pass year 12 grade and got admission to do Bachelor of Commerce (B.Com). As I mentioned earlier, I chose B.Com because I knew a couple of people who had done it. I didn't like a single lecture, but I kept going because it was during that time I was introduced to a thing called the Computer. I remember vaguely that it was a DOS machine, with a keyboard attached. I didn't understand what it was and what it could do but it certainly made me curious.

So during the day, I was doing B.Com and in the evening I was learning more about computers. I was also learning how to use the keyboard, DOS, and Windows. The only other machine I had used before this that had anything similar to a keyboard was a typewriter, which I used to play on in my mother's work office. It felt so surreal.

Technology and the field of computers became very vast and the use of computers in our everyday life increased my interest to study more about it. Learning things that are interesting seems to be more fun and is also easier to understand. While at university, Google and other tools were not available. Computer skills were learned through practise or reading books. Commonly used computer interface was command prompt and the commands to execute a particular task had to be memorised.

I completed my B.Com just to have an authentic degree but my interest for learning computer skills never died. In fact, it was during this time that I acquired most of my computer skills. It is true what they say "One can go to any limit while fulfilling his /her interests".

Soon after, I moved to Melbourne, Australia and started doing Masters in Business at Monash. After a year, I later changed to Masters in IT because the curiosity for technology completely took over during this time. During the final semester of my Masters, we were asked to work on a project which we could demo to the entire class. I chose to design a job classified website, similar to seek.com.au these days, but way before seek widely available. I got High Distinction in the subject but didn't commercially release the product, instead made it available to the university to use for free.

Despite the fact that I had degrees in the business sector; the curiosity and interest of computer remained in my heart. I continued to learn new tools and technologies. These technologies have allowed me to work for prestigious and reputed multinational companies. I have been in the IT industry for many years now and taken on a diverse array of roles from technology consultant, operations manager to an architect and now a leading business strategist in Australia.

I got interested in Blockchain in 2014 after hearing a Billionaire advising us in a seminar to take a look at this new technology called Blockchain as this will change the future.

When I started to research about Blockchain, I couldn't find much on the internet so I started to spend more & more time reading about the start-ups using Blockchain Technology and their documentations.

I started to visit blog sites in my free time and understand the process what makes some of the project stand out, and what makes others not only like them but vouch for them on the internet even though they are not core part of the team.

This is when I started to understand more and more about the way businesses will get transformed in coming years.

I started to share my knowledge on the internet, in the forms of webinars and live events. More and more people joined my workshops. There was a time when more than 500 people registered for my Blockchain webinar and I had to increase the limit of my GoToWebinar licence. In last few years, thousands have attended my online and live workshops

BLOCKCHAIN SECRETS

This book is all about my last few years of journey working as a Business Strategist and Blockchain advisor. Also my research on some of the biggest projects who made it big and end up raising millions in their ICO process

As you may notice, when I started writing this book, it was purely written to help businesses understand the ICO process and what they need to do to be successful in their own ICOs but later this year, Facebook & other social media platforms banned the word ICO, hence, the book name is now changed to Blockchain Secrets (instead of ICO Secrets)

Who is this book for?

This book is a how-to guide for Blockchain Advisors, Blockchain Strategists and Business Owners who are looking to understand what is required to take their Blockchain idea to the market so that they can acquire funding from the investors or how to adopt this technology into their existing business to attract more investors.

Also, this book is NOT a technical How-To Guide on which blockchain technology is best for your business. This book is written to provide you step-by-step guide on what is required for you to be successful in your own ICO process and raise funds. I have reviewed hundreds of ICOs in the last 2 years and found a very specific pattern which makes an ICO super successful and not so successful. This book highlights all those distinctions which you can use and apply in your own business to ensure you have all that it takes to be successful

I would love to hear your feedback about the book and how it helped you in your project, you can reach me via e-mail: support@jagjassel.com

Chapter 1

Blockchain Revolution

Digitalization has created a frenzy in today's technologically driven world. The blockchain is going like hot cakes that has a lot to offer in the field of digitalization, even though it has not been much time since blockchain technology was introduced to the business world. The way we view cryptocurrency, there is no surprise how the blockchain revolution has engulfed the entire technological and business spectrum.

It seems talk about blockchain and cryptocurrency has increased since the last few years. It doesn't matter which industry or business you operate, very soon blockchain technology will affect the entire business landscape. It is important to understand where blockchain is going and how it will help industries and business. In order to understand where this technology is going, we must first understand where it came from – its history. Why? Remember what happened to Blockbuster when Netflix came into the picture? Today nobody needs to rent movies because they can stream the latest flicks on their laptop. What about the taxi industry that was dismantled and overthrown in a few months by UBER? Basically, blockchain is that technology which can make many businesses disappear across many industries. You MUST learn & understand Blockchain and get on the bandwagon before your competition does! However where is this technology headed in the future? In order to find out where a technology will be in the future, it is a good idea to see its past.

The computer world looked drastically different in 1980 than what it does today. A few computers were hooked up with each other – from New York, Boston, and LA to Texas. Just one or two computers hooked together and working today, getting communication done. There wasn't any thought placed on the way computers were built or designed, we just began hooking them up together. Today, the world has become different. It has become more digitally advanced.

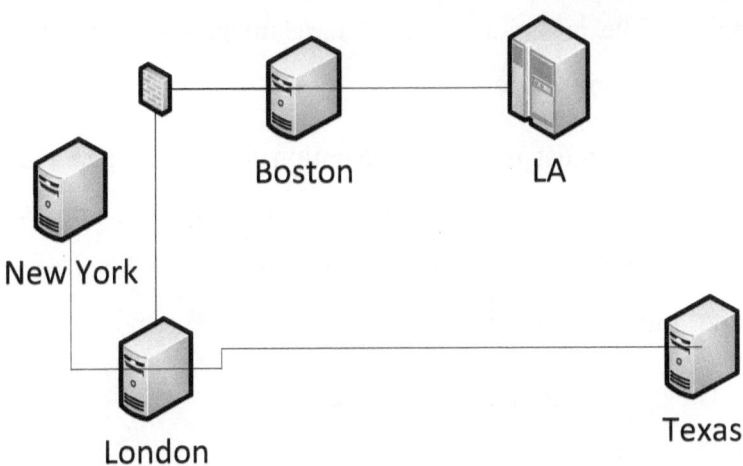

We go on Facebook, click on a link and watch a video that markets a certain webinar. Or you stumble upon a helpful article that tells you all about cryptocurrency, while sitting in the comfort of your home or car. Times have changed a lot over the years. Obviously, it wasn't always like this but we must understand what was it like when not the current picture.

1980 – Era of the Best Inventions of That Time
Imagine what the people must have thought when they say the wheel for the first time. Now think of the reason why it must have been adopted and so quickly by those same people. One of the main reasons why there is mass adoption of an invention is because there is a gap in the

society. The mass adoption of these inventions filled that mass gap in the society.

The first most important invention to fill this gap was the wheel. The second biggest invention was the compass. The printing press was the third most important invention. Other important and BIG inventions were:

- The internal combustion engine
- The telephone
- The internet
- Social media (Facebook, Twitter and other such platforms)

We don't know what will be the next invention but we do know one thing. All of these inventions filled the gap of distance, which was created a long time ago but is now being filled with these inventions. So, now the question arises? Where are the biggest gaps that can be found today? Where is the next major gap? The answer is **TRUST**… which is the biggest gap. As a human quality, trust for us is the most important thing.

As Zig Ziglar puts it, **'If people like you, they will listen to you but if they trust you, they will do business with you.'**

Businesses have been operation since many years, throughout a number of industries and sectors. While we do have a level of communication with them, the one thing missing is irrevocable trust. It makes sense, in order to do business with somebody… it is important to trust that person or business.

Let us consider this example:

Suppose you are buying something online or offline. Out of all the factors responsible for making purchase decisions is trust. You will trust that product or brand, enough to buy it. Suppose you see a product on Amazon and like it enough to buy it… but when you are about to enter your card details, there is a bit of hesitation. The reason for the hesitation? You haven't heard about the seller marketing and selling the product. You won't purchase a good or service unless and until you have heard a lot of good things about that seller. So, if seller is one of the most important things in the world… what is the picture today?

We exchange $100 trillion online per year and buy goods and services. So now you may ask this question, where is the issue of TRUST Jag? We already doing trillion's worth of exchange online. To explain this further, let me take you back to GFC (Global Financial Crisis)

Why GFC – 2007-2008

What has been going on in the business world in the last 10 years? Businesses went in debt as a result of GFC or the global financial crises. How did this happen?

Banks created too much money – financial institutions created huge sums of new money by making loans. In just 7 years, they doubled the amount of money and debt in the economy.

They then used this money to push up house prices and speculate on financial markets. Eventually the debts became unpayable, which eventually caused a huge financial crisis. After the crises, the banks refused to lend any money, and the economy shrunk as a result.

So the question rises, how have we been doing it until today? Let us circle back to trust. You won't buy anything from a random stranger because you don't trust that person.

BLOCKCHAIN SECRETS

It is as simple as that. What we did to get around was create mediator companies i.e. the middlemen who help us complete our transactions. This is the main reason we even have banks! It is these middlemen companies who have all the information on their ledger about transactions between the seller and the buyer or end-user.

This means these companies can also change or add entries into the ledger, from whence the real mess comes. What is the fix? It is called blockchain, a type of ledger through which everybody that is part of the chain can hold the information. This means only one person doesn't hold all the information but many at the same time. What if somebody wants to update or change an entry on the ledger? Consent will have to be asked by everyone else who is part of the chain. Additionally, an invisible entity ensures all entries written on the ledger (of bought products) are right and not made-up. This kind of regulation is called decentralized regulation.

Cryptocurrency is based on blockchain technology, which has proved to be more useful than any other new-found technology. Like any other technology, people were a bit skeptical when it came to investing in cryptocurrency, yet blockchain technology stood on a strong ground as far as advantages to industries are concerned. There is a lot the business world needs to be thankful for as far as this technology is concerned. This revolutionary technology offers many benefits, including digitalization, security, high transparency, and permanency.

The giants such as Google and Facebook, as well as many others, mine the users' data. This is carried out via tracking the data which helps to structure 'Artificial Intelligence Algorithm.' These companies use mined data, save them in their servers, and earn millions without parting the fair share of the amount with the user whose data is used.

Moreover, the start-ups such as Synapse utilize the combination of blockchain technology and AI for data compilation, in an interactive way, generating small networks where data is stored in a decentralized form (using blockchain). This data is then used by businesses and various governmental departments. The users i.e. contributors of data are rewarded for the sharing of their data.

Blockchain In Healthcare

BLOCKCHAIN SECRETS

We have got to admit this fact that the healthcare sector across the world has been degenerating as each year passes. In my country we know that the Govt. is pushing to put the Medicare records on a centralized database. In the US EHR (Existing Healthcare Records) is a system where healthcare data is stored. Quite frankly, the EHR or any centralized database is simply an inefficient and insecure data storage system. The data that is stored within the system is far from secure. Additionally, data entry is an incredibly time-consuming process as well as prone to errors. A likely solution to the above disastrous issues is possibly an Ethereum-based blockchain network called Iris.

Cryptography is used to create records, which are digitally stored in the form of blocks and put on a decentralized platform. This helps to make the data easily accessible to patients and doctors, and also increases security due to the tamperproof feature that blockchain provides. Additionally, the data being uploaded and stored is incentivized. The uploader is given tokens, called Iris tokens. This system helps make the stored data more secure and approachable for purchase by health insurance companies and researchers.

Financial Services

One of the most popular applications (and ultimate launchpad) for cryptocurrency in the global economy is the financial industry, without any doubt. Although today's banking systems are more sophisticated when compared with past systems, yet there are many issues the current systems struggle with. The main issues are that current banking systems lack inclusion and fairness. To explain the dilemma better, interest rates and transactions are heavily lopsided in favor of financial companies. In fact, the customers i.e. those who should benefit the most from banking systems gain little from their interactions with banks.

This situation is made worse when we note how important banking services are, yet individuals are forced into unfair deals. Additionally, there are billions of people in the world who have no access to a bank at all. This is an even worse circumstance. The situation can be rectified at a universal level with the help of cryptocurrencies and blockchain. Anyone can utilize banking services using a smartphone and an internet connection (both are widely available), start a business and begin receiving payments.

Financial services on blockchain technology will place the power back into the individual's hands, with the help of incorruptible ledgers and no centralized authority for oversight. Additionally, solutions will be offered without charging exorbitant interest rates and middleman fees.

Digital Advertising

Digital advertising is a massive revenue-generating stream and is expected to grow even bigger in the years to come. It is the primary form of advertising that makes sense because today people spend more time on their phones and laptops.

The case with advertising, which has been the point of contention since the sector was first established, is to reach an audience and have the power to influence them. For decades, this can be only done by those with the largest amount of money. On the other hand, a lot of issues arise with this monopoly, a centralized advertising power, which is just one of many. Users are often bombarded with irrelevant and frequent advertisements. Data is collected and then exploited to further target individuals. And lastly, little (if any) revenue goes to the individuals whose online content is used as advertising platforms.

Basic Attention Token, a blockchain-based platform is aiming to make this system fairer for content creators. This platform hopes to change the above issues by letting users pay their content creators on a subscription basis as well as provide the option of receiving advertisements.

Credit

Many words have been said lately about the disruption of the money business by blockchain technology, yet the economy of credit and debt is similarly disrupted. Here, Blockmason comes to the rescue. It is a project that establishes a credit and debt platform. The platform seeks to bring blockchain to one of the biggest components of the economy – credit flow that is estimated to be around $5 trillion in value. Additionally, the platform plans to use the Ethereum blockchain in the near future which will create a credit and debt ledger that features smart contracts.

These are just a few examples of sectors and industries that are transforming for the better with the help of blockchain technology. However, we can safely conclude that this technology is still in its early stages and there is still room for industry insiders to figure out even more ways in which the technology can be merged with how industries operate.

The year 2017 saw a dramatic rise of interest and speculation in crypto and the blockchain technology. Even today, a lot of people are wondering what can be done with this technology, how advantages can be gleaned to the fullest capability from this amazing technology. Most people still do not see the practical purpose of blockchain technology. The good news is that there are many new ways the business landscape is being changed by the blockchain revolution. The following are just some of the main trends to keep an eye on.

Blockchain Is Changing New Technologies

The technology world loves new sectors. Some early innovators have already begun to look at how blockchain can influence these budding ventures. A lot of work has already been done from improving legacy infrastructure to creating decentralized markets for APIs. In fact, it has been fully explored how blockchain can play a role. The IoT or Internet of Things has been an early favorite out of all the new innovations in Silicon Valley.

As noted by Statista, an estimated $284 billion was spent on IoT in 2017, soon becoming to be a booming industry. Blockchain technology is set to help IoT devices connect better now and in the future. Although it is still a bit early to say anything with conviction, there are a few firms that are looking forward to making their mark on the relationship between IoT and blockchain technology.

Next Big Thing, a German-based organization, is dedicated to accelerating the development of IoT ventures. Many of those ventures rely on blockchain ledgers to share and distribute information. NBT boasts of a wide array of game-changing applications, which successfully leverage IoT-to-blockchain architecture. Decentralized solutions are delivered to some of the most pressing health and security problems.

The CFO of NBT is eager to oversee continued decentralization of markets through the implementation of this technology as blockchain enables talented and forward-thinking innovators when it comes to building scalable solutions and watershed business models.

A New Frontier For Fundraising

The introduction of the ICO (or Initial Coin Offering) is one of the most exciting blockchain developments. According to Coinschedule, ICOs accounted for nearly $3.7 billion in fundraising for early-stage blockchain companies, which surpassed the total amounts invested in previous ventures.

There are presales of tokens or coins that can be used on whatever decentralized platform the blockchain company is creating. This thinking is different from the traditional viewpoint on investment. ICOs behave similarly to IPOs i.e. it is a public sale of a company. IPOs are for a stake in the company, meaning they are a security. On the other hand, ICOs sell a coin or token to be used on a decentralized platform. This means we cannot be sure whether the coin's value will increase or decrease.

Keeping Information Consistent

As is stated above, the sharing of information within the health and security industries is fraught with discrepancies. Approximately, 86% of mistakes that are made in healthcare are administrative, as a lot of hospitals work on different systems and have a hard time sending medical records with any degree of accuracy. This is exactly what blockchain technology is going to change. This technology's strength within the medical records industry is both safety and security, as well as the speed at which files can be sent. Additionally, it is entirely possible to have a universal identity (like a social security number) that is easily transferable from one care facility to the next, with the help of a unique ID for each patient.

Not only the medical sector, other industries such as financial and security information are also ready to get the ball rolling when it comes to implementation.

Faster And Cheaper

Remittance

Blockchain technology is incredibly helpful, especially in the remittance industry, particularly through the trading of Bitcoin and Litecoin. Remittance is essentially the sending of money from one party to the next. This process can be quite costly in certain places, especially in developing nations. Remittance costs an average of 7% of the total money sent, according to the World Bank. This cost adds up quickly for those individuals who are constantly sending money back and forth.

Blockchain technology has already helped with this area by cutting cost. There are still a few reasons why cryptocurrency has become such a popular choice to send money. First, a coin's value is dictated by the market cap, and not a central government. Secondly, the interchange fees are relatively cheaper, especially when compared to traditional channels like Western Union. Last but not the least, level of security provided actually helps to prevent fraud or theft from an account. Undoubtedly, this is a huge help for places that have poor banking systems.

# Blockchain Technology, Reigning Cryptocurrencies, And The World Economy

Blockchain technology along with cryptocurrencies like ETH and Bitcoin is expected to revolutionize the world's economy. Work has already been started to make this endeavor come true, with numerous ICOs being launched on a yearly basis. However, only a few get close to succeeding. In fact, out of the hundreds of ICOs that are launched every year, about 90% have failed.

The top five Initial Coin Offerings and their respective market cap are:

ICO	Amount Raised	Dates	Project

BLOCKCHAIN SECRETS

Filecoin	$257 million	08/10/17 - 09/10/17	Decentralized Cloud Storage
Tezos	$232 million	07/01/17 - 07/14/17	Self-Amending Distributed Ledger
EOS	$185 million	06/26/17 - 06/18/18	Smart Contracts
Bancor	$153 million	06/12/17	Prediction Markets
The DAO	$152 million	05/01/17 - 05/28/17	Decentralized VC

The past 1000 years have witnessed an incredible advancement from building a wheel to the Internet 3.0. Blockchain technology has risen in the 21st century, being used by various industries such as real estate, finance, and healthcare as well as a few more. Today, the ICO model has become a successful venture used by thousands of small businesses and startups.

The blockchain is used to fund ongoing operations. Regulators have recognized the power behind this idea to collectively mobilize retail investors' unused cash. Institutional resistance is diminishing, leaving established corporations to raise money for their own blockchain solutions. As such, many have already jumped on the ICO bandwagon.

The Blockchain Revolution Is Here

This technology has turned the entire concept of crowdfunding upside down, even if the revolution was a bit slow. From Bitcoin, blockchain technology rose to prominence, all thanks to Ethereum which helped disrupt transactional business processes with a new breed of smart contracts. A new trend in crowdfunding began called ICO because of this impetus. Initial Coin Offering helps new startups to source liquidity.

The concept of crowdfunding has come a long way. By contrast, it is now synonymous with websites such as IndieGoGo and Kickstarter. What do these platforms offer? They provide room to display business plans, product imagery, and organize online credit card and bank payments from interested contributors.

The following are some big shots in the business who are doing wonders with this technology, revolutionizing the way ICO is used.

Kodak

There is a way for large companies to fund an entry into the blockchain space. These organizations can easily capitalize their market presence with the help of an ICO. Kodak has taken center stage for doing the same thing after years of leading and falling behind the camera and photography industry curve.

The launch of KodakCoin is a precursor for all the good things to come to the company. The token will be used to drive a platform that tracks and monetizes image ownership and usage rights on the internet which is an incredibly useful idea. The company has recently filed with the SEC and begun a licensing arrangement with partner WENN Digital.

According to the agreement, WENN Digital has paid Eastman Kodak a non-refundable $750,000 licensing fee for the rights to use Kodak branding on the company's DRM platform. The digital rights management platform will be secured by a blockchain, featuring a native cryptocurrency.

Additionally, Kodak also received 50,000 shares of WENN common stock, a package that is worth approximately $1.25 million. The filing agreement also agrees that Kodak will receive three million KodakCoins at the conclusion of the token sale as an advance payment against its royalties. The assessed value of the tokens does not exceed $3 million at the very least. Kodak will receive three percent of all tokens that are created above that mark if WENN decides to issue more than 100 million tokens.

Sears

Even with all the knowledge backing this concept, ICO is currently viewed as a 'gray area' fundraising model. This is true even after the largest companies are trying to figure out how their tokens comply with the SEC's myriad definitions and standards.

At the moment, ICOs are helping raise billions for small and large companies alike which is the exact same route Sears is taking. One of the company's strategies for digging itself out of financial degradation is to launch an ICO. This is a serious incentive and case for Sears, considering that the company stands as the best candidate for an ICO for several reasons. Firstly, the parent company of Sears and Kmart has shed hundreds of millions of losses in the past years among a series of asset sales, store closings, and declining revenue. A successful ICO-financed loyalty program could possibly help alleviate the company's decline by driving more customers to the brand with the lure of cryptocurrency. This is often viewed as an alternative investment. Additionally, the loyalty program will be funded by the traders of its tokens, which means Sears will effectively receive a discount marketing campaign for absolutely free.

Ask.fm

The question and answer platform Ask.fm is an exceedingly popular internet destination. On the platform, visitors can ask questions and read answers from people using the platform all around the world. This is the simplest idea but with an underlying value that blockchain can really bring out.

The ability to follow users and perform thorough searches means those with expertise can quickly find questions they are qualified to answer in the first place. Users can even ask questions directly from the most expert and knowledgeable parties.

Whispers going around the company are saying that there could be an upgrade soon. In fact, signs are pointing to a looming ICO in the near future. A mysterious AskFM 2.0 has started showing up on the official website with little additional information. However, rumors say this development could involve some sort of token-based incentive system. Theory-wise, providing a cryptocurrency could possibly lead to a better quality content and attract even more users to the platform.

Telegram

The telegram was the first company to come out with a mobile chat application in an age where privacy was scarce. This wonderful application allowed users to easily talk with one another from anywhere in the world, without the fear of having their conversation unencrypted, stored, or shared with any third-party or even governmental influence. The company witnessed its fair share of flak for their refusal to share data with governments, but that did not stop it from using blockchain to improve security and introduce a safe payment functionality.

In the near future, the company plans to launch a chat platform with cryptocurrency payments, which will be called the Telegram Open Network. The TON is also the name of the token which will be generated during their upcoming ICO, which may raise as much as $500 million according to some reports. In fact, this could become one of the biggest ICOs of all time.

Overstock.com

Chief Executive Officer of Overstock Patrick Byrne has taken some really successful decisions during his leadership at the big eCommerce retailer. The most notable decision made is in regards to the acceptance of bitcoin as a payment method. This was done back in 2014. The choice was a good one for the company which has earned billions due to bitcoin's increasing value while overseeing a stock boom. The efforts to turn this company from a retail company into a blockchain powerhouse are continuing to creep upward with the upcoming ICO, which is due to raise over $250 million to fund a new platform and cryptocurrency called tZERO.

All of the above featured platforms enables a reconciliation of digital records regarding just about everything, in real time. In fact, very soon billions of smart things in the physical world will be sensing, responding, communicating, and sharing important data – doing various jobs from protecting the environment to managing our health. As a result, this Internet of Everything needs a Ledger of Everything. Additionally… business, commerce, and the economy most definitely need a Digital Reckoning!

So why should you care, as am innovator and entrepreneur? We believe the truth can set us free and distributed trust will profoundly affect in all walks of life. Suppose a consumer wants to know where that hamburger meat really came from and what other food chains use the meat in question. Perhaps an immigrant has become sick of paying big fees to send money home to loved ones and want nothing more than an affordable system in place. Maybe an aid worker needs easy identification of landowners land titles so it will become easier to rebult homes after an earthquake. Or maybe citizens become fed up with the lack of transparency and accountability of political leaders and want a system in place that makes voting for the right one easier.

Even as I write, many innovators and entrepreneurs are building blockchain based applications that serve all of these ends. And... this is just the beginning!

In this chapter, we have discussed about the blockchain revolution in general along with the benefits of implementing blockchain in healthcare and financial services. We also talked about how blockchain is changing the new technologies and what are the top 5 biggest ICOs in the world. Before the conclusion, it became evident that blockchain is a great step towards the modern day economic revolution since it is beneficial in terms of keep information consistent and providing faster and cheaper remittance.

Chapter 2
Overview Of An ICO

Cryptocurrencies are the latest sensation in the financial world yet this trend did take a few years to get a popular head start. Bitcoin is the first digital currency of its kind, launched in 2009. It is a digital currency based on a distributed ledger technology named blockchain. What does this digital currency do? This eliminates the need for centralized intermediaries such as banks and credit card companies when making electronic payments.

Besides bitcoin, the most popular digital currencies floating in the market are:

- Ethereum
- Ripple
- EOS
- Bitcoin Cash
- Cardano
- Stellar

- NEO

Here the question arises. How are these digital currencies or coins introduced in the market? So, let us take a look at that.

ICO

ICO stands for initial coin offering. The term refers to the unregulated raising of funds for any cryptocurrency venture. Basically, ICOs are one of the popular mediums through which cryptocurrencies enter the market. In retrospect, ICO can also be used as a fundraising tool, used primarily by startups working on new blockchain projects.

An ICO is similar to an IPO. However, there are some differences. An ICO provides a chance to trade future cryptocurrencies against crypto-coins that have a current liquid value such as bitcoin or Ethereum. In fact, most new digital assets and currencies are mainly traded against these two big currencies. Some popular terms for ICO are crowd-sale, crowdfunding, and token sale.

The first ICO was launched by J.R. Willet in 2013 and it took another year, during the launch of Ethereum in 2014, for an increase in funding using this technology. ICOs hold immense importance in the world of blockchain and cryptocurrency, mostly due to the incredible usefulness and growth opportunities for small businesses and startups.

Importance Of Icos For Small Businesses

Businesses used to face a lot of trouble in the past as far as funding was concerned. Perhaps the biggest impact of ICOs on the business scene is the way in which startups can now be funded. A remarkable and significant shift can be seen from IPOs and other more traditional venture capital models to the innovative ICO model. This gives way to liquidity and growth capital, with a shift of focus from equity holders to token holders.

It is incumbent for everyone in the business world to jump on the bandwagon becoming early adopters of the next thing in the cryptocurrency world. A frenzy has been created, where startups are literally bolting a cryptocurrency token to their business model and selling it to investors. On the other side of the coin, it has become a lot easier for a number of entrepreneurs to secure funding for their projects with the help of ICOs. However, stringent regulatory and statutory measures that are required to be checked-off for venture capital fundraising have made it difficult for many promising projects to see the light of day and completion.

ICOs are effective in fundraising efforts, considering entrepreneurs can just go straight to people like us and convince them to invest in their ideas and concepts.

Origin Of ICO

The first reported ICO was conducted by Mastercoin in 2013. The fundraising event ran for almost one month, where Mastercoin raised close to 5,000 bitcoins which were valued at around $500,000 at that time.

As expected, there has been a rapid increase of ICOs since the first introduction. Now, a new ICO is launched every other day. In 2016 alone, 54 major ICOs were raised close to $103 million, with ICONOMI ($10 million) and SingularDTV ($7.5 million) being the frontrunners. Even the previous year has been phenomenal for ICOs, raising around $1.25 billion in 92 ICOs. Bancor and Tezos are among the top ICOs of 2017, with the earlier raising $230 million and the latter raising $153 million. Overall, ICO has raised over $1.3 billion for blockchain-based startups. The crowdfunding technology is called everything from 'revolutionary' to a Ponzi scheme.

In the real world, companies can always secure funds by approaching angel investors and venture capitalists. However, by doing that, they would have to give away a share of their equity to them. What companies wanted was to get a lot of funds without giving away equity and ownership. The only way this could be done was by going public. This was done by holding an IPO, also known as an initial public offering.

What is an IPO and how does it work? In an IPO, a private company basically decides to put its private shares up for sale to the general public. Anyone anywhere can buy the shares of the company. Initially, these shares are dirt cheap and if the company hits big, then there is a chance of an individual's shares increasing to exorbitant prices. An IPO is basically the distribution of shares and other investments. This technology works well under a centrally regulated corporation.

People in the business world thought, 'What would happen if the same concept was used and placed on a blockchain based environment?'

This is how the concept of ICOs was given birth, considering both IPO and ICO are pretty similar except for the following.

Decentralized Authority With ICO

This means there is no centralized authority to regulate the entry of digital currency and ICOs.

ICO Lacks Tedious Red Tape

One of the many reasons why IPOs did not work out is that the tedious red tape that bogged and held back down most IPOs.

ICOs Are Unregulated

This is the most important reason why ICOs have become more popular and useful in today's digital landscape. IPOs have always been under heavy scrutiny and regulation while it is the opposite for ICOs.

However, there was a problem faced by blockchain-based companies when it came to ICOs. In an IPO, the investors got shares in return of their investment. What would a blockchain-based company give away in exchange for capital? Hence, the blockchain equivalent of a share had to be invented. This is where the idea of 'tokens' was designed.

What is the difference between a coin and a token? Coins are used for the transfer of money whereas tokens can be used to transfer ownership of almost everything. Tokens can be used in business for digital objects, cryptocurrency, verifiable voting, etc.

Let us delve deeper into this concept.

What Is A Token

It has been established that an ICO is a sort of mixture between an IPO and a crowd-sale. Companies interested in a particular project in the blockchain can gain access to it by sending the developing team some amount of money, usually paid in Bitcoin or Ethereum, and getting the equivalent amount of tokens in return.

Tokens have gained even more importance and prominence since the advent of Ethereum, which provides a sustainable platform where the blockchain technology can be used not only for making currency but also to make decentralized currency. However, tokens that are native to their environment must be used if using DAPPS. Generally, tokens fall under two categories.

- Usage tokens
- Work tokens

Why ICOs Fail Sometimes

Last year, many ICOs were announced and launched in the market yet only a few that actually made it into the market achieved their goals. The rate of failed ICOs is incredibly high when compared to the successful ones. Launching an ICO without conducting the proper research is a wasted opportunity, something that should not be done in the first place.

An ICO-based company should know what the current standing is so that goals can be achieved and they can stand tall in the market against successful ICOs. Are you thinking of launching a new ICO in the year 2018 and beyond? It is important to have proper planning, research as well as a good strategy to market the ICO.

Also, it is important to seriously consider the reasons for ICO failures. Below are some of the major reasons, including how they can be avoided.

Inadequate Product Market Value

About 80% of ICOs fail at the initial stage because their services or products do not have any value or demand in the market. Therefore, it is important to make sure that an ICO has an audience that needs the offering even before launching and announcing the news.

Most of the ICOs today require selling token to raise the capital. It is important for such ICOs to be registered with the SEC and other related regular bodies so that they can protect themselves from long-term failure.

Additionally, it is essential that the people who are launching the ICOs should have a defined market which is completely aware of the project. Moreover, it is imperative to build trust and reputation to make the ICO into a successful venture.

Failure To Create Brand Identity

People are not brand conscious. They often invest in a project that sounds good but they forget it should look good as well. This factor of failure includes every element of websites such as content logo, visuals, fonts, ICO white paper as well as a selection of fonts etc. The people will question your brand if the website is unprofessional or found lacking.

In a world where more emphasis is placed on aesthetics, how can people forget about marketing and branding of the ICO website? The face of your offer is your brand. This is why it is very important to spend quality time, effort, and resources to create the brand identity. If done a good job in this area, this will lead to many other communication and marketing aspects in the future.

Unrealistic Objectives And Budgets

It makes a lot of sense. New businesses face difficulty due to the unrealistic budgets and objectives that are related to the vision and mission even before their beginning. The higher objectives are set, the more budget will be needed to achieve those objectives. You will also have to spend equally on the marketing, PR, development, design, and content.

This can be avoided easily. Make sure your objectives of offering match the scope of your project. Is your team small for an ICO? It is ideal if you conduct a private sale first before going to the business sale.

Lack Of Audit, Reporting And Measurement

The majority of ICOs that have failed so far were launched by newcomers who had very limited knowledge of the online marketing techniques. They did not understand the need and importance of continuous auditing, measurement, and reporting to improve their ICOs.

This also can be easily avoided. Make sure you know about the tools that can help with the above as well as the tools that help with conversions and user behavior tracking.

Remember that ICO is like a product or service that cannot survive until you are marketing it the right way. You need to understand who your audience is, how to find them, and then convert them to make your ICO successful.

How To Run A Successful ICO Venture

The first requisite of running a successful ICO venture is to decide which platform should be used to launch the ICO. There are many different platforms mentioned above. Once this is decided, you must figure out how you will actually offer the tokens to the public.

There is no standardized or 'right' way to do this. Every token sale model has its strengths and limitations. Therefore, you must analyze your own organization's goals and find the best one according to the information.

The following list of models is by no means exhaustive. Additionally, there are many different variations possible for each listed model. An important note over here is to clearly note down whatever model is chosen and other decisions in your organization's whitepaper or ICO *document* prior to the sale. Now, what is this *document* about? No aspect of a cryptocurrency project is more representative of its worth than its whitepaper. The document acts as a symbolic milestone as well as a carefully designed objectives layout. Undoubtedly, the whitepaper is one of the most critical aspects of a blockchain project as it comprehensively sums up the goals, techniques, processes, and resources necessary to run it successfully.

The following are the four most common distribution models used today.

Capped Fixed Token Sale

- Tokens are offered on a first come, first served basis.
- Number of tokens available for sale are predetermined.
- Price for a token is fixed.
- A cap exists on the total amount raised, calculated by the number of tokens for sale by the price per token.
- Insiders have predetermined tokens allocation which is expressed in the whitepaper.

This is the most common token sale model with many variations on the market as well. For instance, discounts to the token price are often offered to early participants with the price increasing gradually until all tokens are sold.

The total sale duration lasts for one month or until the hard cap is reached. What about unsold tokens? They are distributed or kept by the development team as defined in the organization's whitepaper.

What happens when the soft cap is not reached? In this event, any tokens received as contributions are returned to the supporters as defined in the whitepaper.

Uncapped Token Sale

- There is no limit to the number of contributors and the amount of capital raised.
- Insiders are allocated a fixed amount of total number of tokens.
- Buyers can contribute fully as they choose the project.
- Each token's value is unknown but becomes known after the ICO is completed.
- Anyone can participate in the token sale.

In this model, the ICO-based company can sell as many tokens as people are willing to purchase. However, the percentage of the tokens available is limited. Additionally, the number of tokens allocated to an investor depends on how much they support the sale. The real percentage of tokens for sale and the cost per token are not known until the sale is completed. This can possibly aid in any funding issues for an organization and also attract a huge amount of attention and public pressure.

Capped Auction

- A variable amount of tokens is sold.
- This model can be utilized as a Dutch auction.

- Only a capped amount of funds can be raised.
- A total number of sold tokens are variable, depending on the price paid by contributors.

In this model, contributors only bid the amount they are willing to pay for the tokens. In this case, the development team does not determine the price of the tokens but the market itself.

Let us talk a little about the ICO development team and its significance.

ICO Team And Its Significance

Having a good and experienced ICO development team will pave a smooth way for ICO success for your organization. This is especially true if you are not a developer. A good ICO startup team is at the core of any project, which is why its formation must be carefully considered.

Why is it important to hire a good development team? Without one, it will be impossible to implement and promote even the best idea.

In theory, a potential blockchain developer should have significant work experience in *C/C ++, Python, Go, Java, etc.* More importantly, the professional should know how and when to conduct an audit. The world of blockchain and cryptocurrencies differ from the usual programming language. This is why an expert is needed in this area.

At its foundation, ICO projects need people who have the necessary skills as well as basic knowledge of IT technologies, blockchain development, marketing, and investor relations.

The reason why ICO projects are created and launched is that the organization wants to achieve a certain goal. Imagine you have an idea and its implementation is useful to a particular consumer group. It is important for each team member to understand what the project's vision and goals are in order to better implement the idea.

Coming back to the model, the idea behind it is to incentivize people to *wait* to buy the tokens. In theory, the longer you wait, the higher chances are of a thing becoming cheaper. So, this will insure that there is a mix of people who are willing to purchase at the sale's beginning at the higher price and a group of those willing to take the risk of the tokens being sold. This model promotes the idea of an even distribution of different types of investors across the board.

The last model discussed in this chapter is:

Uncapped Auction

- No limit to the amount of funds raised.
- The market determines the price of tokens.
- Insiders are allocated a fixed amount before the sale.
- Buyers bid for the tokens at a self-chosen price.
- Tokens are sold to the highest bidder first, then to the next highest bidder, until all tokens are sold.

There are a lot of similarities between this model and the capped auction model. However, the main difference is that this model fixes the number of tokens which will be sold. Price of the tokens will be dependent on the price contributors are willing to pay.

How To Choose Your Token Sale Model

There is no perfect ICO model that could make it difficult to make the choice. However, you can analyse your organization and decide which one suits the best and can work out for the goal in mind. Therefore, ask this question. What are the goals and desired outcomes of your ICO?

Some potential goals for any organization may be the following:

- To raise a certain amount of capital.
- To distribute the tokens in a fair manner.
- To enable buyers to purchase set percentages.
- To guarantee everyone's participation.
- To fix a certain percentage to investors and the development team.

Take Note Of Legal Considerations

It turns out the 'wild west' days of the ICO are still here but those are beginning to slowly fade. Almost every major country in the world has begun to introduce legislation on ICOs. China, for instance, even went for temporarily banning ICOs altogether until a way is found to regulate them.

Each country will have different rules and regulations. This is why it is important to conduct proper research. Only then can an organization uncover the laws relevant to your organization and the country you are operating in.

The rules and regulations for the U.S.A. are as follows:

- The SEC (Securities and Exchange Commission) announced on July 25, 2017 that the independent agency would consider DAO tokens as securities. In December of the same year, it released a statement to warn consumers of the dangers of ICO. Such announcements imply that increased regulations are coming. The U.S.A.'s security laws are the vaguest and the most frequently enforced among all the security laws in the world.
- The laws of most countries generally offer clear lists of the type of investments that apply to which types of laws. However, in the U.S.A., 'investment contracts' must follow different laws depending on what type of investment they are classified as. What does this mean? Even though your organization is listed outside the U.S., you are still going to have to play ball with the SEC.
- There are two predominant schools of thought regarding how to deal with the SEC. One is to insure that your token does not pass the Howey Test, which would, in essence,

force you to treat the token as a security. The second way is to assume that the SEC's regulations will apply in your case, therefore insuring complete compliance with laws comes knocking.

The Howey Test

This test was created by the U.S. Supreme Court to decide whether certain things should be considered an 'investment contract' or not. This is a standard test to check if an investment in a business will provide profits to the purchaser, based entirely on the efforts of others.

A recent change to the law has ruled that Ethereum should not be considered a security, while DAO tokens still are.

The SEC is in charge of regulating the financial markets in the United States. It also has jurisdiction over new ICOs when there are investment products sold to American consumers. Organizations that fail the Howey Test are subject to the same regulations as public stocks. They must follow strict securities laws. For most companies, let alone blockchain, the financial and logistic burdens of creating a compliant and publicly traded security are high. The companies that wish to launch an ICO first have to clearly pass the Howey Test.

ICOs are the new seed-funding. In fact, this year will see more start-ups wanting to inch their way gradually into the ICO framework. This development will further embed cryptocurrencies in the financial world.

Yes, shakeouts and changes to the market are inevitable, especially when it comes to paying taxes, but this is the start of an incredibly egalitarian fundraising model and ideal for new ventures. It is important to keep in mind that running an ICO-based platform is a fulltime job for a team. It cannot be handled just by one person. All of the explained elements are crucial to get right, something that the investors will base their decision from. To the entrepreneur, marketing is the most important thing (something we will discuss in the coming chapters). So, having all of these elements in place and understanding the up-front step that will have to be hurtled when doing an ICO are just the first part of being ready. Operating an ICO platform is a demanding job, a long journey of several months (at a minimum), and one that will most probably include a lot of ups and downs. I hope the chapter was able to provide readers with a more solid foundation to understand what they will be getting into and what to expect.

Through this chapter we have talked about the overview of an ICO, focusing on all of the fundamental of ICO. They will undoubtedly help you in understaning the importance of ICO in small businesses and also the origin of ICO to make it easier for everyone to understand the basics of ICO. The chapter further discussed the decentralized authority with ICO, ICO lacking tedious red tape and ICOs being unregulated. The chapter concluded by describing two main factors: why ICOs fail and what is a *"Token."* Few other aspects of the chapter such as the Howey Test were also discussed to ensure every concept embedded in this chapter is clearly understood.

Chapter 3

Vision

Blockchain startups are starting to land funding and pop up in the tech press yet these businesses are light years away from hitting the mainstream. The hype around blockchain is at its highest pitch, so is this the right time to think about starting a blockchain venture?

The answer depends on the venture. The fact of the matter is that blockchain is not a business model. It is just a process for collecting and storing data that fits a certain, and somewhat limited, set of cases.

Ask 10 different people what they think a blockchain startup is and you will get 10 different answers. So, how to decide if it is worth starting a blockchain business in the first place?

Blockchain As A Digital

Currency

Are you thinking of creating a digital currency? You are going to be walking a fine line between an uphill battle and a slippery slope, in such a case.

Creating a digital currency is technically a blockchain venture because the digital currency is an application of blockchain technology. In fact, many people tell that there is no visible difference between blockchain and digital currency. They are mostly wrong. However, it is easy to get the lines blurred. There is a chance that you might be creating your currency on existing blockchain tech or you might even be designing your own unique blockchain. Ultimately, the value of your product will be determined by the value of your coin or token, not by your blockchain tech's value.

Now, creating your own coin is easy. Even launching your own coin as a digital currency has low barriers of entry, evidenced by the sheer number of altcoins out there and the plastic-wrapped thin documentation and technical foundation of some of them.

The battle for legitimacy will be hard-fought. The coin is quickly becoming regulated, with its impact still relatively unknown. 80 ICOs have been issued in the past month in the U.S. Additionally, digital currencies are subject to SEC regulations. This means that most coin operations need to enlist good legal help.

Consider an existing business plus blockchain. It is often recommended to add blockchain to an existing business model but it is also correct that blockchain cannot be just thrown at the wall to see what sticks. The entire business process needs to be revamped and everyone within your company reeducated.

There is a little pressure to insure everything is done in the right manner, at the first time. Lessons from the recent past show how difficult this kind of transition could be.

In the mid-2000, when the entire business world shifted from client-server to web-based application architecture, behemoths like SAP and Oracle began losing their enterprise dominance to companies like Salesforce. The rest of the businesses innovated too little or too late, which is why they eventually went into obscurity.

It is hard to learn this lesson apparently because the same thing began happening all over again in the 2010 - this time with mobile-first development and Software as a Service (SaaS).

- Step 1: Blockchain
- Step 2: To be determined
- Step 3: Profit!

Read up articles on tech websites, all you will find are the titles and content that are a variation of "Startup X is using blockchain to change the way we think of Y." Where Y is education, non-profit, voting, gaming, food sourcing, healthcare, home buying, legislation, grocery shopping, travel, social networks, entertainment, and so on. All of the above are fine things to change. In fact, there is no need for entrepreneurs to always start with a painful problem and then finding an innovative solution.

There are many reasons why innovation must always be a solution-first game, as long as you go back and find a painful problem to solve afterward. Here is how this can be done.

Firstly, blockchain technology should not be used to solve a problem that does not exist in the first place. Make sure there are enough people with a real problem who are also looking for a solution. Only then will people be ready to pay more than what it costs you to solve the problem.

The next step is to make sure the scope of the problem is narrow enough to keep your efforts focused. For instance, education is a huge problem in desperate need of many fixes, but blockchain is not going to fix all the problems present in this sector or even some of them. Implementing blockchain may fix one problem, which is why it is recommended to focus on that.

Finally, make sure this technology is the right solution. So, where should you start? Simple…

Start At The Beginning

In a few words, blockchain is the storage of data in a block, which is then chained to the next block. It is much like a snake of data. There is nothing new about this. What is a technical breakthrough is the part where machines can spin through cryptography at a scale that makes the chain possible. The magic and the real deal in a blockchain startup is the application of transparency, security, and efficiency of the blockchain model. Additionally, there are elements of automation, speed, and verification in the technology that are relatively new breakthroughs, which make the digital currency a possible concept. Yet, this is just the beginning. There is so much more that you need to look at when thinking of starting a blockchain business.

Need For A Blockchain Business Startup

Like any business, your blockchain business needs well-defined goals, ideas, and objectives. ICO can be considered one part of the blockchain business but not the only goal. This is the mistake most businesses make. They make the ICO the only goal for their blockchain business to be successful. For businesses looking to enter the blockchain fold, it is no longer enough to have an enthusiast, who drives awareness and adoption of the technology. Focusing on a specific part of the business might leave other areas of the organization out of the loop. Therefore, it is essential to think about blockchain in a more holistic and strategic way to get the best from this wonderful technology. The first requirement is to get organized. Ask these questions:

- What is your business' vision?

- How does blockchain technology fit into that?
- What is your timescale for adoption?
- How do you drive cohesion among different lines of businesses?
- What does this technology's implementation mean for your infrastructure?

It is a good idea to consider the role you wish to play as an entrepreneur within the emerging blockchain ecosystem. For instance, companies are now forming a rage of consortia just to drive adoption and innovation as well as innovation. Should your business also join any or do you want to lead a consortium? What about creating your own blockchain for an area of business? You can also decide to use another company's. These decisions should be taken early on the process as this will bring other parties on board as well.

The next step is to scope all available opportunities. You must have objectives. Scoping the opportunities helps to figure out how to meet them. Do you partner with a large tech organization or a specialist startup? Will choosing a specific line of business help leverage blockchain to transform a current business?

Have you identified a way for blockchain to create an entirely new revenue stream? Many businesses are in the middle of deciding to take advantage of the up-and-coming 'business as a service' model. The right route taken can depend on the use case. In the end, whichever model is chosen depends on the set strategies and goals.

The third step is to successfully assess what your business needs in order to meet set objectives. The question that must be answered is: Will you require outside skills that help unlock value from new solutions?

In such a case, you need to consider upskilling current staff, as this is essential. Educating your staff in-house will go a long way when it comes to redressing that imbalance. The last step is to be flexible and adaptable considering blockchain integration solutions, with the existing business process, require adopting a certain level of flexibility. One way to insure a smoother transition and integration level take place is to create trial processes in a sandbox environment.

These processes can easily be co-created as well as new models that work together if other parties have bought into the project of an earlier stage. Only then can they transition to real business processes when everyone is ready.

From there, it is often a case of learning as you go. There are still many things to consider, such as creating management and governance processes and assessing your current business controls. Approaches to managing blockchain projects throughout your business are fluid.

All of the above are detailed with the help of whitepapers and roadmaps. A whitepaper will describe the ICO in complete detail as was covered in the previous chapter. This document tends to focus on the problem at hand that will be solved. Moreover, the white paper will list down the goals, objectives, and future plans of the company. On the other hand, the roadmap describes the timeline of your ICO. It will describe each stage of the project from its initial phase.

The following are some essential steps that can help make a strategic plan for ICO startups if implemented correctly. The most important is:

To Identify The Goal

Understanding the business model is really important before initiating the development phase. Additionally, it is crucial to understand various elements, challenges, and objectives. Some other external factors such as market competition, trends, and opportunities should also be kept in the mind. The costs and benefits of the project should be measured and weighed, with the expected efficacy analyzed. How does this help? This will enable them to establish whether the investment is actually a worthwhile endeavor or not.

Other steps to be taken are:

- Visualize a use case.
- Choose a suitable consensus mechanism.
- Select an appropriate platform.
- Design the architecture.
- Configure applications.
- Build the API.
- Think about admin and UI design.
- Enhance the applications.

A basic model of the blockchain application can be outfitted with futuristic technologies. Some of the technologies that can be integrated into the application are artificial intelligence, machine learning, bots, cognitive services, cloud, data analytics, and the internet of things. However, there is not only one recipe for a successful integration of blockchain, as shown by the following biggest ICO success stories.

Ethereum

This is a public, open-source distributed ledger platform that allows users to create smart contracts as well as decentralized applications.

Vitalik Buterin launched the project in 2013 and since then, it has grown into one of the largest blockchain projects on the market. In fact, the platform has attracted a lot of attention from a wide number of industries due to many reasons. Primarily, the platform can be potentially used to digitize and streamline insufficient business processes in the future. This is one important reason why the platform's digital currency Ether has achieved such an amazingly tremendous increase in value since it first launched.

Initially, in 2014, the Ethereum project sold 11.9 million Ether tokens to raise $16 million. Ether's issue price, at the time of the crowd sale, amounted to $0.311. As the second biggest digital currency on the market, the all-time price of Ether has been $1,431.77. How has this digital currency been so successful?

The ICO platform was built to allow for the development of decentralized applications and smart contracts. Both have the potential to become revolutionary technologies in the near future, not only for the private sector but also the public.

Storj

Undoubtedly, Storj is developing a next-generation decentralized cloud storage solution that pays users hard drive space who rent out their spare to other users of the network.

The Storj token has actually been around for a lot longer than many others. The token began to trade in autumn 2014, after the first ICO event where one token was sold for $0.009. Today, this token is worth $0.631, with an all-time high value of $2.96. How did this come to be?

Storj was among the blockchain startups to provide decentralized cloud storage. Growing popularity of the cloud as well as an incentive mechanism that paid users in digital currency, this platform attracted a substantial investment. Its first ICO was conducted in 2014 when the company raised about $461,000. Then in 2017, Storj managed to raise three million in seed funding and a further $30 million during a second token sale.

Monster Byte

This is a cryptocurrency gambling platform where gamblers from all over the world can bet on sports or play games like Roulette and Blackjack.

Monster Byte first announced its pre-sale on July 6, 2017. It sold out completely in five minutes at a price of $0.11 per token and sold about 2.5 million tokens. An ICO was launched two days later which also became a quick success, selling over five million tokens during a general sale.

According to the CEO of Monster Byte, the only reason it was successful in such a competitive ICO landscape was its uniqueness. It had already been an established company, operating in the cryptocurrency landscape since 2013.

Additionally, the ICO company came up with a well-though-out capitalization opportunity, which insures anybody who invests knows what they are getting into from a financial perspective.

Kik

Kik is a messaging app that raised almost $100 million in ICO, insuring one of the most successful results ever in the history of ICO.

It was somewhat unusual for an ICO, seeing Kik is an established business, nearly 10 years old, and has over 15 million monthly users. Additionally, the business value amounts at more than $1 billion. The business could have easily raised venture capital but chose against going this direction, picking an ICO model. In the end, this decision turned out to be the right one.

Kik is serious about its cryptocurrency called Kin, short for Kinship, as far as vision goes for the company. Its ultimate vision is to be one of hundreds or thousands of digital services for Kin. The idea is to integrate Kin so well that consumers could easily earn and spend this digital currency at all the preferred places. Although this seems like a bold vision, Kik is quickly becoming one of the major players in the ICO landscape.

MobileGo

In late April and from May 24, 2017, GameCredits held $53 million ICO. The company is well-known for creating the first mobile gaming store that accepts the digital currency.

50% of the earnings go to marketing out of the $53 million raised. Additionally, investors can possibly gain exposure to the mobile gaming market by obtaining MGO tokens. The mobile gaming market is currently the fastest growing segment of the global games market.

The MobileGo whitepaper states, *"The mobile gaming market was $36.7 billion in 2016. As per current growth rates, it is expected to grow from $58 to $58.1 billion by 2020."*

Even though the MGO tokens have been distributed, investors can learn a thing or two from the GameCredits offering.

For starters, ICOs like this provide opportunities to profit from high-growth sectors such as the mobile gaming industry. However, the use of these tokens has not yet been proven so they are speculative assets. Another way of putting that is investors should not put any money they are unwilling to lose in such assets.

The above ICO success stories could not have been possible if the vision was blurry. This is why it is important to highlight a good vision first and foremost. Creating a short statement basically guides a company for the next three to five years. However, the vision needs to be specific enough to say something about what you will do and equally what you will not do. The vision of an organization should be capable of driving it toward achievement of a common goal. Having a vision also offers a constant reminder of what you are trying to achieve when the going gets tough.

More importantly, the corporate vision of your ICO should tell the investors everything they need to know about the objective and mission a company will achieve. Am example of a good corporate vision is Google's which is, "to provide access to the world's information in one click."

The company's nature of business is a direct manifestation of this vision statement. For example, Google's most popular product is the search engine service. With the help of this product, people can easily access information from around the world. The company applies its vision together with the mission statement to maintain dominance as an Internet technology, software, and hardware business.

A business without a vision is like a ship without a rudder, in constant danger of drifting aimlessly. Many blockchain businesses do not have a clear vision, meaning they jump from task to task without having a clear understanding of what actually connects individual actions together. It is difficult to discern the level of value created by those individual actions. Take a leaf out of the above examples and implement – watching investors and users connect with the business on the highest level possible!

Throughout this section we have shed light on the vision of the blockchain starts up and blockchain as a digital currency. The main factors consisted of the steps that include starting at the beginning and need for a blockchain business startup. Few others factors included the identification of the goal, introduction to Ehterum (crypto currency) and several other applications to conclude this chapter.

Chapter 4

Whitepaper

One basic requisite of running an ICO business is writing the white paper. Why is this piece of document important? A white paper is basically an authoritative report or a guide that informs readers concisely about a complex issue, presenting the issuing body's philosophy on the matter. A white paper is meant to help readers understand an issue, solve a problem or make a decision pertaining to an issue.

In simpler terms, a white paper can be taken as an instrument, a document that helps a business explain themselves to people (mostly investors). What is shared in the white paper? Information like what problem is the ICO business solving, how are they solving it and what is their course of action to achieve the same is found in the piece of document. Additionally, salient business issues are addressed, products are showcased and a competitive solution is given an outline for easy reference.

The common and major four reasons of writing a white paper for your ICO business are:

- Vision of the project
- Sharing technical knowledge
- The problem faced
- Generating publicity
- Distribution of business information
- Attracting prospects
- Core team and their track record

In the previous chapters, we discussed briefly what an ICO white paper is. According to www.nasdaq.com, an ICO is "A fundraising mechanism in which new projects sell their underlying crypto tokens in exchange of bitcoin and ether. It is somewhat similar to an IPO in which investors purchase shares of a company."

2017 was the year that saw multiple ICOs across the globe. Even the first quarter of 2018 successfully raised millions of dollars via ICOs. However, not many were as legit as previously expected... especially the ones that came before 2017. This means people found great difficulty in understanding what an ICO is really about.

At its essence, every legit ICO should include several elements, a white paper that explains why the company is raising funds needed funds, being one of the essential elements. As a token buyer, the most important thing when it comes to investing in an ICO business is to understand what it does. This can be only understood by reading the white paper even if the business highlights a brochure, website or infographic video. The idea isn't to simply cover the basics but indicate the genuineness of the startup. A white paper can be of multiple types, as well for a single ICO. Some are written to explain the economies, some written to explain the business and tech and some simply with the marketing or PR aspect in mind.

There are some white papers that also mention disclaimers about the risks involved to investors when investing with the startup. Such white papers that relay all the risks involved wish to let investors know of the complete picture. Doing so inherently increasing trust of the community in the business. In the end, these papers definitely inspire pre-ICO sales and make the ICO a successful one.

It is therefore really important to design and create the white paper explaining the workings of your ICO business, correctly. In order to create an attractive and informational white paper for your ICO business.

How To Create Your Own White Paper For ICO

All it takes to write a good white paper are the following parts:

Project Outline

It is crucial to get the project outline the first time. What does this part in the document include? The project outline should clearly define the exact problem you intend to solve. The key to making the project outline is to ensure it is unique and catchy.

In fact, the project outlines needs to stand out from the crowd, prompting investors to read more of the document. What do you need to remember when creating a white paper for your business's ICO project? The average investor reads about hundreds (if not thousands) of whitepaper outlines every year, which is why most just get as far as the project outline.

The Solution

In every document, there is always a section present that is the soul and glimmering hope of the entire document. In the case of whitepapers, the solution is that section which can help make the project shine!

What does the solution section include? It should include a thorough breakdown of your project, including a complete project description that shows exactly how the outlined problem will be solved by the project's implementation.

As a result, the section needs to include a detailed market analysis data to show exactly what is needed for the solution and how it fits into the preexisting marketplace.

Obviously, most companies usually have only an outline or prototype of the project they wish to undertake. In this case, you should include as many of the visual data or mockups that you can to help investors easily visualize your project.

Detailing how the budget will be broken down is a good way to reassure investors about how you intend to spend the money. This will help with further evaluation of the project plan as a whole and also convince investors that your ICO isn't a scam.

Another thing is needed to be included in this section, which is some form of development roadmap. What will it do? The developmental roadmap will help give investors an idea of where you see the project heading, reinforcing their confidence that your business understand the marketplace even prior to entry and investment.

In the end, it is crucial to make this section stand out. Try to emphasize the unique selling points of your project.

Detailed Explanation Regarding Token Release And Marketplace Considerations

You need to give a breakdown of your ICO token issue as well as evaluate market considerations. This section includes details regarding your crypto tokens, including their value, how many you intend to use, and which crypto token platform you intend to issue them.

Another important point to include in this section is how you will allow investors to redeem their tokens. The section will also provide details on what happens if your ICO doesn't reach the funding targets outlined, which is called the investor refund process. Additionally, this section will also include your terms and conditions or an easily accessible link to your website where the above information can be found.

Finally, the section must also include the relevant security details that will help investors determine if your ICO is safe. You can also include information on their company should you choose to employ a specialist security firm to launch the ICO. Remember, no matter how attractive your ICO might seem to investors… no person on this planet is going to pay for digital tokens if they believe there is a good that of the transaction being unsecure.

Entire Team's Overview

Why is it important to write down the entire team's overview? Including the profiles of all the different team members really helps to increase investor confidence and interest.

The current market demands the support of certain individuals from within the blockchain community, as this can guarantee an ICO success. However most ICOs don't have the necessary support of such individuals, yet investors want to see who is involved in the project and what their backgrounds are, before investing.

Does any team member in your team has a background that includes a successful ICO launch? If yes, then you should definitely include this information in this section.

Remember, the important part here is to convince your investors that the project has the passion and technical knowledge to succeed.

Besides the essential components of writing an ICO whitepaper, you must also take care not remember that there are some risks involved. Those risks are of a regulatory nature, financial, business as well as security. Let us discuss in the following:

Regulatory

A definitive ruling on ICO tokens and investments hasn't yet been issued, which is the reason why there is a lot of speculation in the market. The main question is which token sales are subjected to securities, regulations and how these rulings might possibly impact noncompliant startups.

The safest investment route to take in simple and straightforward. Only invest in startups that conduct their ICOs in direct coordination with legal firms and restrict token sales to accredited investors.

Business

Majority of startups fail although ICOs provide these startup businesses with the opportunity to raise capital that is needed to launch their projects. This must be realized by investors, the sooner the better. This risk can be easily mitigated after businesses consult in-depth ICO research reports such as those published by Strategic Coin – before it is time to make an investment decision.

Financial

ICOs remain highly speculative, even in the current market. This means investors must be prepared to face volatility and potential loss. Here is where an ICO whitepaper helps the most, by stating an impressive return target. However, this is a goal and not a certainty. Once again, risk can be mitigated by investors by consulting in-depth ICO research reports and only investing in startups with an experienced team and a cogent business mode.

Cyber Attacks & Fraud

Finally, it is crucial for investors to remain vigilant when it comes to avoiding falling prey to cyber-attacks. Crypto-finance is a burgeoning field without clear regulatory guidelines or even best practices. Moreover, cybercriminals are always on the lookout to steal funds from investors.

One of the most common attacks are phishing scams. In this kind of attack attackers impersonate another individual (such as an ICO's founder) and deceive that individual into sending them (the attacker) their funds or providing personal information.

As with everything that needs to work, there are some mistakes that are conducted when designing an ICO project. The first one is:

Not Defining Your Target Audience

A crypto-savvy community already familiar with the basic technology was targeted by early day ICOs. Obviously, the most heavily laden whitepapers in tech-speak earned credibility in the crypto world. However the ICO market soon saturated, meaning the crypto world is now mainstream. What does this mean? An ICO's project's whitepaper has to cater to a wider audience of future token users, many of whom aren't even crypto-savvy.

It means a lot to the prospects of your ICO if the whitepaper is targeted to a broader audience, yet it must be clearly defined and written with them in mind. How much do they know about technology? How much explanation is required of the target industry? Ignoring these questions and more means you run the risk of over or under explaining important facets of the project, which will alienate the reader. Dive into the mindset of your key target demographics and explain the project in simple and easily understandable wordings, without leaving important details.

Not Identifying Why The Project Needs A

Blockchain Or Token

A few years ago, 'decentralization' was the magic mantra for a successful ICO. Now the landscape has thankfully matured and readers will want to know why an idea or product will benefit from being decentralized. Does the blockchain add a key piece of the puzzle that no other solution will complete? Does your token achieve something specific that a token or coin already existing won't? Having a well-thought and developed answer will assure contributors that you HAVE thought through all the details.

Underestimating Importance Of Your Team

Many don't realize this but their background, experience, expertise (as a whole company) are actually more important than anything else when it comes to success of a project and token sale. Not only do ICO participants want assurance about delivery on the promised product. Additionally, a good team's portfolio will reassure token buyers that you won't be usurped if someone with more experience or insider knowledge comes along with a similar project. Think about these questions: Does your team include the right subject matter experts in your team? Do you have the right sphere of influence? Do you understand your market? Do you have what it takes to pivot, if it is necessary? When considering this, always go above and beyond the list of companies or projects where ever you have worked. It is a good idea to include details on how long you have been involved in the industry, entrepreneurial experience and why the project was created in the first place.

Failing To Tell A Story

In essence, the whitepaper should be a document that relays more than a series of facts. If there is nothing included except hard facts and numbers, the readers will grow dull and bored while reading. Omit long paragraphs from the whitepaper where ever possible and enlist the help of bullet points. Please don't forget to add your 'who, what, when, where, and how'.

Example

The blockchain captures prescriptions from doctors so everyone can see them at any time. Instead of this line, try:

Our platform captures each patient's medical prescriptions on the blockchain, giving care providers a record of current medications in emergency cases where the patient isn't responsive. This record is permanent therefore opiate abusers will have a difficult time getting prescriptions from multiple or even new doctors. This will place us at the forefront of the war on opiate addiction.

Think about which project would you prefer supporting?

Burying Readers In Buzzwords

Sometimes, the whitepaper is filled with certain keywords or buzzwords that supposedly capture the attention of readers more quickly, relaying the importance of a certain news. Take the following example in consideration, where the buzzword is obviously 'decentralization'.

"This revolutionary solution will disrupt our industry. All users will be able to access a decentralized network by decentralizing transactions on a distributed ledger. Other advantages will be globalization of the industry and

incentivizing our users with a 2-sided marketplace in this billion dollar industry. Did we mention it is decentralized? Because it is decentralized."

Many whitepapers face the same issue, getting deeply entrenched in rhetoric that they forget to actually say anything. The paragraph above doesn't explain why someone should invest or contribute to your project. Instead it has a lot of white noise and unnecessary words along with the company's voice which can also get muffled. It is also a good idea to avoid saying statements that are overly grandiose. Think back to the grand and absurd statements used in the example. Are you really disrupting something or did you simply invent a new and different way to achieve it? The reason Starbucks is insanely successful and popular today is because the coffeehouse has developed a different way to approach coffee, focusing on the quality of the coffee beans. By being upfront and avoiding overstatements, a lot of trust can be built between you and potential token buyers.

In conclusion, a whitepaper is the perfect tool by which vision, passion and ambition can be shared for the project – with those who would like to invest. However the real struggle lies in writing this piece of document in the right way. In such a case, your project's whitepaper will not only attract participants but also supporters invested in your blockchain project's mission.

This chapter, whitepaper, described the steps on how to create your own white paper for ICO and defined basic explanation regarding token release and marketplace considerations. In addition to that two major factors were also incorporated *'Not defining your target audience'* and *'not identifying why the project needs a blockchain or token.'* The last factors of the chapter included failing to tell a story and also burying the readers in buzzwords.

Chapter 5

Website

There are a number of things that can affect An ICO launch including the ICO website, technical aspects of SEO, the technical setup of the ICO, community-related issues, public relations and the overall SEO strategy. Additionally multiple are interrelated factors are concerned with the success or failure of an ICO's marketing strategy. It is equally incumbent for an ICO website to hit its token sale targets, in order to be called a profitable ICO campaign.

This is why the importance of website for your business's ICO launch cannot be emphasized enough. However it must be remembered that the ICO must rely on its website and not solely on the actions of distributes, exchanges, or agents. Additionally, the ICO website must also be structured in such a way that token sales can be generated just as consistently post-ICO. SEO is touted as one of the best ways when it comes to achieving long-lasting results with token sales and ICOs. In fact, cryptocurrency and the blockchain which it is based upon benefits a lot from an optimized marketing campaign. Marketers and ICO specialists consider this to be an effective way to achieve strategic success with investors and the broader market.

Enhancing Blockchain Startups And ICOs With SEO

Many blockchain startups and ICOs miss the mark by a mile when it comes to SEO. This is evident when we see overall poor implementation of blockchain SEO in all the operations that really matter.

It is SEO that lays the groundwork of a strategic growth paradigm for a business. Any entity seeking lasting online success requires a well-structured SEO plan. Even more important, it is absolutely crucial to maintain fully optimized websites after the ICO project has been successfully launched.

Question Of The Day: Are Blockchain & ICO Companies Preparing For Post-ICO Growth

There comes a time when any startup that barrels through the ICO phase of their business's lifecycle, hits a critical stage in operations. The first indicator of this is a significant volume of capital is generated from the token sale which is used to fund business operations.

Many people don't realize this phase of business operations can see rapid growth and development for the company if the necessary technology is in place. However things look significantly different from an insider's perspective. There tends to be short-sightedness when it comes to ICOs, especially when a business only focuses on getting their tokens to market and raising capital.

What needs to happen instead? Long-term viability of a brand and the digital company's blockchain technology must go further beyond the realm of ICO. Work should be conducted to ensure capital raised through an ICO is essentially put to effective use.

There is another reason why blockchain technology is an incredibly hyped up concept. Smart contracts and decentralized technologies are the way of the future, so questions are raised about how the company wishes to conduct its operations, manage its product lines, and position itself for the future.

These ambitious objectives can be achieved easily, however the company's advisory boards, marketing management, and top-level leadership needs to direct operations accordingly. What more needs to be done? Brands launching their ICOs need to demonstrate strategic vision and growth prospects. Even though the importance of implementing SEO strategies in ICO launch is considered important in its own right, one question still crops up.

Are Website Consideration Necessary

After 3 Months Of ICO Launch Date

Believe it or not but a business launching an ICO project shouldn't even think of adopting a short-term approach to their blockchain marketing campaigns. Launching an ICO should be taken as a long-term investment which is promoted by building a company that generates the necessary capital even after the project's end. Other operations can also be conducted such as sustaining growth operations and ultimately becoming successful in the endeavor.

It should also be remembered that technology takes time to build, implement and generate returns. A company can thrive only if its ICO is launched on a well-developed and thoroughly SEO-optimized platform.

Despite the growing importance of having a well-optimized website, there are some online marketing professionals have the following notions about creating a website. They think that:

- Technology offered by blockchain and ICO companies doesn't need a website presense

- A blockchain and ICO company doesn't need to focus on the ICO launch website as a strategic asset

Besides this, a well-designed website can provide potential investors with sufficient information that they need about the blockchain and token. It effectively portrays the team behind ICO launch as well as the project details.

Keeping this in mind, attention must be paid when it comes to designing the website.

Factors To Consider When Designing Your ICO Website

What should be considered when designing a website for the ICO launch? Firstly, you should think about who will visit the website. This will give enough direction when it comes to structuring the pages to perfectly align and include visitors in all niches.

Consider the following 3 categories of people will visit the website, to be on the safe side:

- Critics (stray visitors, the government, review websites, ICO enthusiasts and noobs)
- End Users (people whom you are creating the proposed products or services for)
- Investors (people who will buy-in, leveraging on capital investment)

It may sound difficult to include all abovementioned people when creating the website. Yet there are websites that do appeal to all three categories of individuals without giving off bad signals (scams, illegal, or amateur). At other time website design is often overlooked due to inability to understand the importance. It is true that the information found on a platform has a way of speaking to each person in a different manner, according to their objectives.

The idea here to ensure communication is fully tuned to every category of person that visits the website, so that repeated entry is promoted. This can be done by initiating proper design of the website. Some important aspects that need to be worked upon are:

Content

One thing that all websites have in common is content. In fact a website is differentiated by the type of content it features. An ICO platform basically contains the following elements, which provide the least possible information that should ideally be present. The idea here is to convey the most basic idea that is represented by the product or service.

URL – The web address that takes people to your platform should contain a unique and easy IP as well as be eco-friendly. A common practice today is to use .io as the ICO domain extension, which is a cool thing in its own way. Whatever domain name you choose, remember to make it simple, unique and short for investors to remember especially when referring to other people.

Logo – This is an aspect of any website that people see to determine professionalism and legitimacy. As such, the logo design should be mature and communicate value. Additionally, the logo must also relate with the project as well as the audience you are trying to capture. Having good graphic art and well-pixelated logo is the way to go.

Links – All websites have more than a landing (index) page. The other pages showcase:

- An about us section
- Contact details
- Development team profile page
- Links to other documents (whitepaper or technical paper)

Introductory Notes – This section should be simple, objective and informative. The whitepaper or technical paper will contain the detailed explanation of what the project will embark on. However the website shouldn't be scanty. Abstracts from the whitepaper can be used in this section but first simplified and in an orderly fashion.

Important Referential Documents – These are whitepaper, official documents, financial statements, compliance policy documents, partnership agreements and other legal documents which could boost trust. Even though legal documents don't imply regulatory standards in-place, still putting them on the website will help build a reputation for the business even before it starts.

Schedules – The roadmap as well as important dates are pointers that dictate different phases of project development.

- What do they indicate?
- Where you are now?
- Where you will be in the next month or five years?
- What will you will be doing when certain benchmarks are reached?

This also indicates milestones; what achievements you (and the team) have accomplished in the past. How will this information help? This kind of detail is incredibly useful for both startups and expanding enterprises.

Team Structure – A crucial element that needs to be present on the website's page is detailed profile for team members. No doubt, your investors will want to see the faces responsible for launching the project and their portfolio. Additional information on this page could be attaching their LinkedIn profile pages. The idea behind this exercise is to create a good impression to investors.

Communication Channels – What should be found on the website's pages are links to social media, blogs, forums and news or article journals. Investors and supporters of ICO will want to see how relevant the activity is through multiple platforms, from forum talks to hitting major news headlines and regular updated articles that cover the project's progress.

Take the example of ICO Tracker, an ICO website which features the following information through its platform:

- Name
- Logo
- Base
- Description
- Number of available ICO coins
- Date the ICO project started
- Start bonus
- Amount raised
- Links to ICO social media, whitepaper and company website

Layout

The layout of a website is an essential first step when it comes to creating a website. It is the layout that provides structure to a website, just like houses have structure. The layout determines how a website is designed and made.

Elements that need to be taken care of when designing a website's layout are:

Organization – The content on the webpage needs to be arranged and styled properly, in such a manner that promotes user-friendliness and concise communication of intent without obstacles. The following must be considered:

- Column styles; numbers of columns, and how each column relates to the others – flow of information grid
- Outlines and alignment; how the page's content is arranged will present an organized form of thought. This helps visitors find specific information on the platform
- Font style and formatting; attractive web content are colorful, even if reduced to a gray scale color scheme. An ICO webpage must have the right font size, font face and font color
- Images/graphic art placement; a plain website without any multimedia of any kind can be boring for visitors. This can be solved by adding relevant images, graphic arts, infographics and video presentations to spice up the site
- Responsiveness; that time has gone away when browsing experiences were just limited to desktop design. Now everyone has a smart device with them, which helps

access internet information. You don't want to be left out or limit options given to the client when they decide to visit the website. Make sure the website is mobile friendly and looks easily understandable in all platforms.

Color Scheme

Choosing the right colors for your website will make it easier for visitors to read the content. The following needs to be considered:

Complementary Smart Color Selection – The right color and hue blends will create an attractive design, something that a professional front-end designer understands. A glaring color scheme hurts the eyes, causing visitors to spend less time at that website. Similarly, a pleasing and right color scheme will prompt the visitor to read more.

Relativity and Impression – It is crucial to relate your product with a specific color, something which fast-food restaurants also do. However most people omit this very important aspect of the color theme style. Additionally, conflicting colors are also used on each aspect of the webpage (font color, logo and background color). These are all different elements of the web platform and should have contrasting variations in color yet should also be complementary in design.

Additional Unique Features For Website

Editor's Pick

This feature can recommend the best ICOs for investing purposes.

Newsletter

It is a great way to let investors know of upcoming ICOs that might interest them.

Large Community

Utilizing social media such as Twitter to actively encourage investors to interact and share information is a huge selling point.

Chat Feature

It is a good idea to have an inbuilt chat feature on the website and other applications. This feature will help users to share information and the latest hot tips with other users.

Blog Articles

Having a blog and articles section on the website will help with SEO as well as make it easier for users to find information.

Sort By Most Earned

This is a sorting feature that allows investors easy and quick access to only the best performing ICOs.

Mistakes Made When Designing ICO Website

Doing the following mistakes can warrant a poorly constructed website, which can play a large role in the failure of an ICO project. On the other hand, ensuring that following mistakes aren't carried when designing the website will promise success.

Issues Due to Poorly Written Code – Websites face various issues repeatedly due to poorly written code at the time of inception. This can lead to glitches in the smart contract or hackers being able to exploit weaknesses in the programming for their own personal gain. What happens when hackers hack inside a website's programming and begin their exploitation? Cyber-theft is a common issue, where huge sums of money can be stolen. Trust of investors in your company and project is also shaken. At this point, they can question your capability to follow-through on promises with safety and security.

An additional issue that happens is when the platform where the coin is being launched cannot handle the transaction volume that is often experienced during the ICO. This is seen time and again whenever a popular ICO is launched.

It is a good idea to take a series of preemptive actions that will mitigate the effects.

Having Poor Technical Documents and Website – Sophisticated and experienced investors will look at your technical documents or whitepapers to glean an idea of what the platform is trying to accomplish. Today, it is common to see multiple whitepapers explaining different aspects of a project. This is why the document as well as the website must be able to clearly explain the reasons why investing in coins in the first place is a good idea. All the benefits and use cases of the tokens must be clearly articulated. A whitepaper of this nature as well as a professional website are the best tools for marketing the project.

Failing to Market Your ICO and Build a Community on Relevant Platforms – Many companies begin their ICO project from scratch. Success can be assured by taking one important step which is to build trust as well as a following within the ICO community. Nowadays, all that a successful ICO needs is a coordinated and strategic plan to market and increase awareness about a project. What does this step include? Writing press releases, commenting and blogging in Reddit, updating the Facebook page, Twitter account, using Telegram, Slack and Discord etc. It is also a good idea to include easily accessible links on your website.

Finally, designing the perfect webpage for an ICO project can be a big task, requiring specialized skills in both front-end and back-end programming. Additionally, marketing and publicity must also be utilized fully. It is up to how many webpages you wish to nominate to the ICO project, most platforms only prefer a single page design that keeps the audience in one spot while the entire website is perused.

Or you can opt for multiple pages, which is quite effective for the organization and compartmentalization. Whatever the method of organization and presentation intended, the ultimate aim is to bring about the necessary information about your project to the audience and engage them interactively.

The buzz around cryptocurrency and numerous alluring offerings is real and tempting – making it difficult not to act like a popular character in pop fiction and tell everyone to "Shut up and take my money." With this in mind, do not get carried away. Maybe buying isn't your thing, maybe releasing coins is your true path. In any case, if you have a great idea that will possibly make the world into a better place, it is worth to give your ICO idea a try. However it is alos a good idea to enlist the help of a professional team of website developers.

So far, we discussed the effects on ICO websites and enhancing blockchain startups and ICOs with SEO. Several questions were answered throughout the chapter and the chapter concluded with factors to consider when designing your ICO website that includes the content, layout and color scheme. Lastly, we discussed the mistakes that are committed while making an ICO website.It will help you build a better website and can improve the chances of getting more traffic.

Chapter 6
Marketing

The real difference between success and failure of an ICO project is in the marketing. Obviously, just designing and creating an ICO isn't the only requisite considering you will also need the investing world to know about the project! This is where perception marketing comes in the picture. It is essential to plan a winning marketing strategy right from the beginning. In fact, the marketing strategy that will be chosen may possibly be more important than even the actual product. Why is this? This is because while your product may change, the public's perception of your team and project rarely survives a bad first impression. Hence, you MUST create a certain perception in your target market about your brand and business

Additionally, the marketing aspect i.e. the level of efforts put towards this will determine how well the project is received by potential investors or not. This means marketing is one of the most important aspect of building up an ICO project! Yet, not just any marketing works when working on an ICO project.

Why Normal Marketing Doesn't Work

The importance of any ICO project has already been established. A company's entire growth plan depends on the success of this project! Only then will you be able to raise enough capital for your organization.

Another reason why normal marketing efforts won't work when it comes to ICO projects is due to the immense competition. With over 1500 cryptocurrencies in circulation, across nearly 10, 000 markets –ICO and cryptocurrency offers tough competition despite being a new market. This is why normal marketing will never work for an ICO because the technology and concept is totally new compared to the rest. How do you explain a prospective investor the concept of 'contracts' instead of hard cash? Is your prospective investor able to understand what all can be achieved with your token? Can the tokens be exchanged for real money?

Normal marketing efforts won't answer all the above questions. The reality is: different purposes can be solved with the use of different tokens and cryptocurrencies, which can become confusing for potential investors. In the case of money, we know that it can be used to buy stuff. We even know what sort of money a business will accept.

In the case of tokens, different businesses might be accepting different tokens or cryptocurrencies... so your investors might think it is some sort of closed-grouping activity. This can dissuade them from investing. The future of ICO and cryptocurrencies is fast evolving and might not even be the same we are used to in the current time. Additionally, there are many concepts investors don't understand about this... which is why normal marketing will never work.

Why Specialized Marketing Is The Answer

The simple fact of the matter is, marketing for an ICO needs to be a multi-pronged effort. You need to make people aware and informed at multiple levels, throughout the project's duration. In the end, marketing your ICO successfully doesn't only include prompting people to invest in your ICO. Lack of knowledge about basic ICO concepts also makes it difficult for potential investors to go forward with the idea.

The advantage that conventional IPOs have is that people are pretty much aware of these industries and even if they are not aware, there are many mainstream publications that are constantly publishing news updates on these industries. For example, if there is an IPO for a steel company, you know why steel is used. By quickly going through the business pages you will find out whether the demand for steel is going to increase or decrease in the foreseeable future. Accordingly, you can invest in a steel IPO.

For this endeavor, successful ICO marketing strategies and campaigns can be designed, which can prosper with the utilization of a certain number of different marketing campaigns. Running a successful ICO campaign also requires adopting a multi-faceted approach that maximizes limited different resources, using different (conventional and non-conventional) marketing channels.

The fact of the matter is, ICO marketing campaigns need complex promotion methods and strategy elaboration. A competent marketing strategy that ultimately leads to a successful project requires the following elements:

- Correct presentation of the project and problem which it will solve
- Evaluation of competitors
- Preparation of necessary internal documentation
- Taking into account all legal and financial aspects
- Having a strong relationship with the crypto community
- Carrying out technical implementation (from tokens to site development)
- Correctly allocate budget for paid promotion
- Letting marketing managers accompany the project at all stages of the ICO campaign

However, it takes a lot of time for a successful campaign to be implemented after which results can be derived. Time is therefore another crucial element for start-ups. How much time needs to be given? At least 30 to 90 days are recommended to build a strong, active and efficient ICO marketing campaign. Another important aspect to think through is the duration of the campaign. Generally the essential period in the ICO model is the first 24 hours and the last 24 hours.

Roadshows – An Example Of Specialized ICO Marketing

Demand and need for Roadshows in particular attract the majority of inquiries we receive in this ICO frenzy. Roadshows are a great way to increase exposure and link with local partners to gain credibility through network effect.

A roadshow is an intense and effective way to rapidly gain community in target locations. They help propel your project and unite a network with links to investment, future partners and Blockchain enthusiasts as potential community marketers. Take the time to do some prep work, remember your strongest investors are future token holders that believe in your project and make the most of those road shows!

What is the right time to begin marketing efforts?

The Pre-Launch Phase

Ideally, the best marketing plan should start months before the ICO project launches. It is essential to become an active part of the crypto community even while the project is still in the planning stage. Building connections will make it easier to promote the ICO, right at the moment it starts. This is the opportunity to glean information that improves both the marketing strategy as well as the ICO. There is a lot to learn by engaging the crypto community, what projects investors are the most excited about and what marketing efforts seem to really engage them. You should take notes about what does and doesn't work.

Will your project benefit people outside of the crypto community? It is a good idea to spend some time networking with them as well. This is a good way to gather ideas for what problems they have which could be solved by the blockchain, beyond the problems that you have already outlined for your product. So, after building a killer website for your ICO…

Publish On Blogs,

Medium, And Steemit

It is stupid to forget the importance of the written word when working on your website and creative materials. This is where blogging comes in the picture, which is a valuable tool for establishing yourself in the cryptocurrency community. You have the choice when it comes to keeping a blog on your project's website, or if you prefer to submit guest articles of information to well-established crypto and tech blogs.

Following platforms are ideal for blogging:

Medium

Offers a rich source of information for the crypto community. In fact, the Medium community is quite large, informed, and engaged. Publishing (or even commenting on well-read blogs) shouldn't be ignored.

Steemit

This platform is also incredibly popular in the cryptosphere, which lets investors and users share short articles about ICO. In fact, sharing short articles about your ICO project is a good way to spread the word regarding it.

Both applications offers functionality that allows users to 'upvote' content, so it is important that quality content is created. This ensures that people will want to read and share the content with others. What should the articles for these platforms cover in their content? Ideas or solutions rather than just a description of your ICO.

Value Of PR And Media Outreach

It is time to begin reaching out to the public via marketing once the website is complete. There are investors and even the general public that needs to know about your ICO and the solution offered for their problem. A number of options are available to maximize your PR and media outreach.

The first option are press releases, which is a tried and tested method of getting your ICO's message out to the public. There are some top-tier websites that provide their services, publishing press releases but you must build a good relationship with them. Otherwise a premium will have to be paid in order to get the press releases published.

Importance Of Community And SMM For Icos

Two components that promise an ICO's success are social media management and cryptocurrency management. At the crux of it, the crypto community is vast, incredibly knowledgeable, and ever-expanding. All of the potential must be tapped into to achieve the wanted results for the ICO. The priority in this case is earning the trust of the community, which can be achieved by presenting the ICO in the best possible manner. How well the ICO is marketed decides the different trust levels within the community and also become the deciding factor between success and failure for your ICO project. There are a number of verifiable online channels that can successfully promote ICOS, but only a few free marketing channels that are also the best such as:

Facebook Groups – There are many groups on Facebook that regularly discuss blockchain, ICOs, and cryptocurrencies. A simple entry and search will help you find the top used ones.

Reddit – There are many channels within this marketing platform, which are incredibly popular with the crypto community. Exposure can be achieved by simply commenting on existing threads or creating subreddits. You will require a minimum account age and karma, so be ready to become active on this platform well before the ICO is launched.

Telegram

This is one social media channel that shouldn't ever be ignored. A big thing in next-generation community building and messaging, using this platform will market your ICO better than any other. In fact, Telegram has been now embraced by the crypto and blockchain communities for various reasons.

Quora Discussions

This marketing platform has slowly proven to be a valuable channel when it comes to ICO coverage. Threads are updated regularly, which are a great place for a budding and to-be launched ICO to gain needed exposure.

LinkedIn Groups

There are many groups within the job searching site that boast of members in the tens of thousands. It is a good idea to join these groups and being active as well. Joining a LinkedIn group is a good way to connect with other industry leaders and know what is going on.

Specialized Forums

Many popular specialized forums are widely used by the crypto community and can also provide great exposure for the ICO. Just like Reddit, some of these specialized forums have account age and activity requirements. Which is also why it is important to build your presence in the community during the pre-launch phase.

Other SMM platforms that can be put to use are YouTube and Instragram. However, it doesn't mean your marketing efforts won't fail even after using all of the above SMM platforms. In fact, failure of an ICO's marketing sometimes lies on little things that could have been avoided.

ICO Marketing Fails

The point where most ICO marketing fails is even long before it is even launched. This is why a comprehensive strategy must be developed even before it is time to market the project. The first step will be with messaging and then expanding to understanding how it interacts with all of the above.

It is essential to express the project in clear terms, no matter what you are building or what solution you are providing. Make it understandable and relatable to your audience. After all, nothing is more important than the words on the page.

Make sure the chosen strategy is sound by considering the following questions:

- What is the fundamental problem you want to solve?
- What is the pain or issues that the problem is causing?
- Who will benefit the most from the solution?
- How is the solution unique?

It takes the successful melding of many different factors and concepts to run a successful ICO, keeping harmony in mind. By correctly identifying your core audience, the problems they face, and presenting a solution which addresses their pain points, you can fashion a marketing strategy that speaks directly to their needs.

Remember, a great marketing strategy is one that intellectually tempts your audience. More importantly, it is successful in making a deep emotional connection to the proposition. Find that connection first before attempting to tie the open knots of ICO marketing. These days, announcing your ICO is not enough, you have to go an extra mile to receive

substantial investment. Theses marketing tactics will create a buzz for your ICO to attract more

investors. You can use the available platforms to raise awareness of your ICO such as bitcoin talk. Reddit and social media are the ideal platforms to market your ICO. Comparatively, Twitter has a larger crypto community. Furthermore, marketing on ICO-specific sites will boost chances for investments.

For most of the time, investors are not concerned about the projects behind the ICO. They are more focused on the flip tokens. Using PR for your ICO will be the most effective aspect.

What is the best ICO marketing strategy? The crypto space is still very early and consumer behaviour hasn't been fully established yet. It is still unclear how people will use cryptocurrencies in their day-to-day lives (considering the applications are many), and how companies leveraging blockchain technology will add value to their users. Despite of that, it makes a lot of sense to get in early on the action – especially considering all the multimillion dollar ICOs that have taken place without needing to go through the process of pitching venture capitalists.

In the end, all you need is a good product, a well-thought-out message, good copy and a good marketing strategy in order to separate yourself from the other companies trying to cash in on the ICO craze, and raise a significant amount of cash in the process. So, what marketing strategy will you choose?

Now you know the different strategies of marketing and also stated why normal and traditional marketing isn't effective at all. Other factors included why specialized marketing is the answer and roadshows (an example of specialized ICO marketing) which led us towards the different phases of marketing and launch of the websites and later on, discussed the value of PR and media.

BLOCKCHAIN SECRETS

Chapter 7

Team

Congratulations! You must have now integrated your ICO into an existing business model of your project if you have come this far in the book. What is the next order of the day? Finding an accomplished team to launch the project successfully! The team MUST include talented blockchain developers first and foremost... these professionals will be able to elaborate project implementation and further development. In addition, they will also be responsible for supplying post-ICO support.

Your ICO team will be an essential component when it comes to launching an ICO project. Ask yourself what makes your chosen ICO team really qualified and valuable for the project first. This is a significant piece of work – a lot more important than researching team members' social media accounts. What are the pointers you need to look out for?

Finding An ICO Team

The first advice anyone with an ounce of ICO launching experience would be to look in the right places when forming your team. A good idea is to explore the top ICO listing sites, track projects, and find out which blockchain development companies are standing behind them. Who knows they just might be a perfect fit for your ICO project!

There are a number of platforms that list down examples of the most trending ICOs that are currently running. Always select the platform that is the most informative and trustworthy.

Another consideration is utilization of global freelancing platforms. For instance, Upwork is a marketplace which encompasses more than 12 million registered businesses and independent professionals. The platform allows you to conduct interviews, employ, and cooperate with freelances and agencies. Additionally, the platform offers a time-tracking application, and takes screenshots while the person is working. An added feature is online chat which helps save a lot of time spent sourcing and hiring. It has become very easy to hire a skilled and right blockchain developer after reading the provided references.

The third and final advice seasoned ICO businesses can provide is to take advantage of a simple Google search to explore new company names.

There are some factors that need to be considered when tailoring your ICO team for the most successful project launch. There are:

Blockchain applications in development require a team with a specialized set of skills. This is a fact, which shouldn't be overlooked! Don't just rely on the description of a team on their website. The company has to be diligent, well-managed, and flexible. All of these skills are those of a good executive. It is a good idea to check management first. How to check if a leader is suited to your ICO project? A good way to validate leaders is to check their personal achievements. Is this their first practical experience in the field? Have they run businesses in the past?

Remember, in the end a team operated by a great leader is always destined to win big! Now that is covered, how much important it is to have a strong management team when it comes to guaranteeing the success of an ICO project?

The managing director of Crypto Asset Management Tim Enneking puts it this way:

"I would rather have an A team with a B idea than a B team with an A idea."

Having strong management teams at the helm of the project is often the key differentiator between an ICO that enjoys wild success and one that falls flat on its face. Thus, an essential element of finding the best projects is investing in ventures that are backed by a strong management team. At least this is what potential investors will look at when traversing the highly crowded field of ICOs.

If only it were that simple… keeping in mind that you will have to delve inside the mind of your potential investor when making your ICO management team. So, the same points need to be followed when making your management team that are followed by investors when evaluating the management team leading an ICO project. Here are some great ways to assess an ICO team you are considering to enlist, which will help you separate the wheat from the chaff.

Check Out LinkedIn Profiles

To make everything easier for potential investors, it is a good idea to attach links of team members' social media profiles on the ICO website. The first place investors will look for evaluation purposes is LinkedIn, which is a good place to start. The platform contains profiles that offer a wealth of information regarding a professional's work experience and educational background. Additionally, this platform is a great place to know the answers of important questions such as:

- Does an individual professional or team have a strong track record?
- Have they generated success in the world of blockchain?
- Is their education what you would deem to be sufficient to bring the project to fruition?

According to managing partner of hedge fund Neural Capital, Ari Nazir observes:

"It is imperative to evaluate if the team has the pertinent experience to what they are building. For example, if you

are building an Ethereum competitor or a stablecoin... your team should enlist experts in distributed systems and/or cryptography. This may seem obvious, but the recent bull market has led to less investor diligence and scrutiny for ICOs as many invest based more on Social Proof and FOMO i.e. fear of missing out than technical merit or product/market fit."

When conducting research on a team, the following should be kept in mind:

- Do they have the wherewithal to ensure that the project's goals are realized? Everyone has ideas, but implementing them successfully is another thing entirely.
- Having a strong track record of delivering is certainly a plus point
- What is the relevant educational background of the team? Have they finished college degrees?

When looking into the background of individual team members, it is very important to take a holistic view, notes

Jessica Ridella, senior analyst for Bitcoin Market Journal. She states:

"It is incredibly important to evaluate an individual's entire experience...I think that experience should comprise of education, field work, and network."

Ridella emphasizes that while a lack of college education is certainly a red flag, "an amazing track record of projects in a particular field" and a "huge network" can make up for this.

ICOs are also evaluated by Bitcoin Market Journal to aid investors when it comes to choosing the right ICO project. The platform has created the Blockchain Investor Scorecard, which evaluates token sales by looking at several categories and giving them a rating between 1 and 5. It is incumbent for ICO businesses to look at these categories and work on them:

- The Market
- Competitive Advantage
- Management Team
- Token Mechanics
- User Adoption

The analysts at Bitcoin Market Journal will ask the following questions after looking at an ICO's management team:

Q – Does the team have a demonstrated track record of success?

Remember that it is the team members who will push your project forward and bring it to fruition. Is the team weak? Or does the team comprise of rock stars that can make things happen?

Q – Does the team have industry and technical experience?

Does the team member have '10,000 hours' of experience in this industry? Are they a group of newbies flying by the seat of their pants?

Q – Does the team, and all its individual members have integrity?

It is important to look further than social media profiles to see what has happened in the news. It is possible to miss key deadlines, for example. They can also claim to have received funding when they didn't in reality. Having integrity is important, so if the individual team members doesn't demonstrate scrupulous honesty and complete transparency, would investors be ready to invest their money?

The bottom line is when an investor thinks of putting money in your project, they are essentially putting their trust in the team that launches and operates an ICO. It pays to make sure you have valid reasons for enlisting the team members for the project. Of course, there are so many other ways to evaluate an ICO team, which should be used when making the team.

8 Keys For Conducting ICO Team Evaluation

An important thing that investors look for when researching about an ICO project to invest in is the project team. An ICO investor will consider whether there are risks or not in investing in a startup. They also have to consider if the venture is honest and authentic, not fraudulent in any manner.

Keeping the above point in mind, i.e. the tips that investors follow to decide whether or not a certain ICO startup venture is a good idea or not, you can also find and enlist the best people for launching the ICO project! You can:

Find Them On Social Media

As mentioned above, it is important to have links to the members' accounts on the different social media accounts for the landing page team board section. LinkedIn is the preferred one, while other social media platforms are also good venues to check if a professional you are thinking to hire is really an expert at the subject.

Visit their pages, read their posts, check the number of connections, personal photos and career ones as well.

Connect With Them Directly

Like investors wanting to know all about an ICO project, similarly you must also wish to know about the team members that will ultimately launch and operate an ICO venture. This must be done before hiring the team members for their designated positions.

A good idea is to observe what happens on common channels like Bitcointalk official threads or Telegram chats. These platforms are mostly operated by community managers and have other ICO professionals who may have the relevant experience you are looking for.

Note The Size Of The Team You Want

There are plenty of ICO projects scattered across the market that are raising tens of thousands of millions while their staff consists of only five persons: two or three chief officers and a couple of technical specialists. That is it!

Even then, the size of an ICO team depends on the type and size of the project that is being launched. Some require lesser people with more concentrated skillsets while other projects may need many more people than just five, bringing with them a variety of skills. In the end, a successful and efficient ICO team comprises of:

- Business Strategist
- Senior Blockchain Advisor

- Market specialists
- PR managers
- Designers
- Legal advisors
- Accountants
- Community managers
- Analysts
- Project managers

Having a small team is acceptable, but only when launching a small budget project. Make sure that the size of the project meets with the size and skillset of your ICO management team.

How Do Team Members Cooperate

How well or badly the team members cooperate and interact with each other means all the difference between a successful project and an unsuccessful one. See how the way your hired team members interact with their peers and how they are physically distributed. Chances are, remote locations of team members can throw a wrench to developments and operations although a strong collaboration process and strategies can fix any communication problems that may arise.

Try to hire team members from the same city, ensuring the higher probability and success of the ICO both during and after the launch. Modern technologies have made it possible for professionals to conduct remote work which means you no longer have a confined list of people you can hire. However big projects are still difficult to administer due to huge amount of backlog of tasks and issues.

It boils up to the situation the same when the left hand doesn't know what the right hand is doing. What happens then? This eventually leads to strategic faults and results in direct damage to a startup's wealth.

Inclusion Of Specific Experts

One thing that is absolutely essential for a specific niche startup team is to have a dedicated specialist on board. For instance, a deep sea research project must involve a marine scientist, so similarly a crypto exchange must have its own crypto traders.

Why does this need to be handled? Keep in mind how every niche is full of its own specific risks, meaning if the team isn't aware of those risks…the project will fall into the jaws of unexpected hurdles. The project will also eventually fail.

What About Project Advisors

Hiring a project advisor is a waste of space in the employee roster as well as a waste of money. In most cases, these specialists just get paid for being shown on the project page. That is all! The amount they receive depends on how much significant and impudent a particular advisor is. Some might gain one thousand dollars, while another might get hundred thousand plus profit share.

What is the job description of a project advisor? Normally they don't take any part in the project, their assistance is limited by permission to use their photo on the project landing page. Additionally, there are a number of fake advisors in the market who falsify their experience to bolster selling to ICO companies for their projects.

However there are exceptions to every case and this one is no different. Hiring a skillful advisor who is also fully involved in the proceedings can possibly give a huge real boost to the project in question.

Experience In Crypto Industry

Without a doubt, this is the most important consideration when making your ICO management team. Having experience is everything in this field. Project leaders, technical experts as well as marketing specialists should have the relevant years of experience as well as be able to demonstrate their proven experience in the crypto area. Why is this so?

The rules in the field of crypto currency are significantly different, and even acknowledged professionals from the traditional economy need some time to get used to the fast and different pace.

Building An International Team

Cryptocurrency is an international phenomenon so it makes sense to build up an international team. There are so many projects that are designed and developed all over the world, in Eastern Europe, Asia, and Africa. Moreover, people from these corners of the world want to explore the many choices out there when it comes to investing in cryptocurrency.

The obvious thing to do is select and hire international team members to cater to outside audience. The first benefit if of course communication. Many people in mentioned regions rarely speak fluent English, which can probably affect international communication. Hiring native English speakers will solve the problem, bridging the international communication gap.

Who should be hired? This mostly applies to marketing specialists, community managers as well as those who are responsible for the project's public relations and relations with investors.

The bottom line is, when someone invests in an ICO project – they are placing their trust in the ICO project's team to deliver on its promises. So, getting together a team which has all the markings of a successful team not only makes sense but it also something that an investor will look at.

The investor will want to vet your chosen ICO team, which is just one part of the process of proper ICO evaluation. Want more information about the other ICO pieces of the ICO puzzle? You can read more about the Bitcoin Market Journal's Blockchain Investor Scorecard. You can also find the most current information available on a variety of ICOs on the initial coin offerings page of the journal.

As you have read through this chapter, you may now realize that finding the team and 8 keys for conducting ICO team evaluation were discussed to drive the chapter further to discussing how team members cooperate and inclusion of project advisors in the team. Lastly, the concluding factor was looking for experienced people in crypto industry and building an international team.

Chapter 8
Minimal Viable Product

It doesn't matter how solid you have designed your business plan or how thorough the market research was conducted. There will always be unexpected surprises waiting at the end of the tunnel when pushing the ICO product or service to a savagely competing market! How can you make sure your product or service has a fighting chance amongst the many ICO projects that are launched nearly every day?

Enter the Minimum Viable Product (MVP) that gives ICO startups a chance to test their product or service in real market conditions before pushing it out in the market for real selling. Additionally, MVP also takes advantage of the everyday consumers and their product buying habits to evaluate the performance of a certain service or product.

What is a Minimum Viable Product and how much important it is when it comes to gleaning product or service performance in the market?

The MVP is a product idea that only includes the necessary features and options that allow the company to release that particular product idea to the market. The product in question is introduced into the market as a type of prototype. This offers many advantages to the company introducing the prototype product, such as product evaluation, reducing cost, and testing the product performance. The MVP can also be introduced in the form of a demo video, landing page, pilot version, or preliminary release.

The important question comes in the mix – how to determine the features that need to be added to the product to ensure successful selling when it is release to the market? Keeping in mind the product must be evaluated prior to being released in the market and not after that.

This varies from one company to another, based on their business plan as well as the budget, product development timeline and of course the nature of the product.

Help of a product hypothesis is taken, which is based on innumerable assumptions of the largest group's demands and usage. However, launching a product just on the basis of assumptions can bring a world of trouble to the ICO venture. This is where the role of an MVP becomes even more prominent.

What Is An MVP

A minimum viable product is basically the first saleable version of your product, which is designed with minimum yet sufficient features before releasing into the market. This product is highly capable of pleasing or satisfying early adopters of the product. Another benefit is to validate assumptions of usability and demand the basis on which final product is designed and developed.

Why Do You Need An MVP

They say an MVP is all about 'Minimum Effort, Maximum Learning'. This concept helps to reinforce the Build-Learn-Repeat Model i.e. you get to first develop a product according to wants and needs of early adopters, with minimal resources and then introduce the product to the market followed by learning what else can be done to improve the product.

Therefore, an MVP lets you test your ideas in the real market as it is a rough but working version of the final product. In fact the prototype product is usually created to check and find real-user behavior with a real product when it is in the market.

What are the benefits of an MVP

Validates Your Riskiest Assumption

Remember that your riskiest assumption will usually be your unique selling proposition, which is validated with the help of MVP before investing everything in a business model (which revolves around it).

Builds a Validated Marketing Strategy

Testing your product strategy with an experimental but viable product will help you to learn most of the characteristics, habits, wants, and needs of your target audience. How does this help? It will become easier to build your final version of your product with a not so likely to fail marketing strategy.

Avoid Overbuilding

Entrepreneurs sometimes include many undesirable features while developing a product hypothesis. The usability and demand for this product hypothesis are validated at the time of the MVP stage. Hence, the final product is built with the aptest features which are desirable in the market.

How To Build An MVP

Let us for a moment suppose an entrepreneur wants to build an e-commerce website that deals with baby products. There are a certain assumptions:

Target Audience: 25-40 old mothers

Best Selling Product: Diapers

USP: The product is delivered within 6 hours

Most Opted Shipping Method: 6 hour delivery

We know that your aim is to build a full-fledged baby products e-commerce store which will be differentiated from others because of your 6-hour delivery but you need to validate your assumption before going all in. You have to validate that if target group actually cares about this USP or not.

The question here is: How can you do that easily without draining your project? The answer is simple…

Just build a one-page website that offers a 6-hour delivery of diapers and collect data of the visitors. The data will include visitors to the website either when they shop or when interest is shown (towards the product or delivery) in order to validate your assumptions. This one-page website will be acting as the minimum viable product for your bigger e-commerce store.

Examples Of MVP

What isn't considered an MVP? Developing and testing just a tire when you want your final product to be car isn't a minimum viable product. As mentioned above on many occasions, an MVP is the minimum but a viable version of the final product which will help you collect the maximum amount of validated learning about customer habits and other important details.

What does this mean exactly? Well, the first thing that comes to mind is that ICO ventures don't really need an MVP to be successful considering there are others ways of finding out customer views on a product than creating a prototype and setting it into the world. However there have also been occasions where an MVP was available and also made a huge difference when the investors could see the demo of the product during roadshows and tradeshows. Repeated testing of the product is the key here… designing a product and then introducing it to the world doesn't mean a product has to be perfect. It is crucial to test the product before moving towards final launch. Taking the customers feedback to improve the product can also make the vital difference when developing the final version of the ICO product.

The Unusual Truth about

Why an MVP Alone Won't Make You Successful

In the startup world, 'failing fast' is the Holy Grail. How to succeed? Pivoting is the only way to reach success! However we see so many startups fail and pivot in such stupid and dumb ways. Yes, failing often is another way to find success eventually but this doesn't mean you cannot fail smart. Actually, in order to do well in the world of ICO you need to fail forward!

What that looks like visually? This is how most startups pivot: Failure is the only thing that follows from failing without making progress. Why does this happen? Because they're drinking the startup kool-aid. They're stuck with the MVP-idea. They're stuck in the Build-Measure-Learn loop.

"The most important thing to test your assumptions and pivot."—Nearly everyone into startups.

However there are two fundamental flaws with the above thinking:

Innovator's Bias

It is a natural and common occurrence to come up with problems around our brilliant ideas, and then try to find just enough evidence to convince ourselves we are on the correct path. This is known as the innovator's bias.

If you have thought about starting with product testing, the first thing that needs to be determined are the actual problems. Doing this becomes very difficult because of this bias. We are hardwired to recognize fake problems around our solution, which increases the odds that we will convince ourselves to be on the right track. This is exactly the thing you want to avoid!

Lack Of Flexibility

It is really difficult to recover from a test that invalidated an assumption, if you start with a problem that doesn't exist. Flexibility of the project can be damaged and ruined if the entire problem isn't explored. This will make it difficult to extract actionable problems from an interview.

So, when starting out on the product development... you need to maximize learning and minimizing the time to get the right product-market fit. Instead of building your MVP as soon as possible, it is a better idea to start with a minimum viable understanding. What is MVU?

This means going back to the initial steps of creating and launching an ICO venture i.e. the pre-ICO development period:

- Presenting an ICO idea to the public
- Writing a white paper
- Compliance with legal requirements
- Attracting ICO advisors
- Creating a token
- Advertising the campaign

The project is ready to be launched only after settling all of the above steps. Holding an ICO means beginning the crowdfunding process, for which supporters can invest their funds into any such project (with acceptable cryptocurrencies) in exchange for project tokens. It is also important to keep an eye on security and make sure the website is stable and safe from the attacks of scammers.

Post-ICO Development

Period

When the project collects sufficient funds according to the goals set in the white paper, the following steps are performed:

Using The Tokens

In this phase of post-ICO development, investors can either save their tokens for the future (in order to sell or trade them on exchange later) or use them within the project (if this is expedient).

Developing The Product

This period consists of numerous actions to push along the product; run the tryouts; improve security within blockchain technology; continue promoting post-ICO public relations; and conduct ICO marketing. It also includes social-media management to keep investors informed about the relevant situation.

Often, when reaching the soft cap, developers stop being active in certain areas, as they think the crowdfunding period is over. This can result in negative outcomes, as post-ICO management is just as important as the previous stages. Let's have a look at the post-ICO review in detail to understand its necessity.

Post-ICO Review: Key Steps To Follow

The post-ICO development period is the terminal part of conducting the campaign. Its main goal is to deliver value and the final product to the customers (token-holders). In the end, company tokens aim to be listed on exchanges, so investors can easily take part in a token sale or exchange, process payments or deposits, and, of course, get their profit.

It is important not to underestimate the necessity of intelligently performing post-ICO strategy. Otherwise, even after crowdfunding, a company can lose money or clients, or receive negative feedback. During the post-ICO, it is essential to follow the roadmap milestones step by step, with an explanation for each.

Let's take a look at the main post-ICO development goals.

Post-ICO Public Relations And Marketing Strategy

Post-ICO public relations between the team and investors is one of the priorities both in pre- and post-ICOs. All investors should continue receiving newsletters highlighting current news and updates. Social-media management is an integral part, as well. To communicate with investors and establish favorable public relations, it is highly beneficial to use such channels as Slack, Twitter, or Telegram. Post-ICO marketing strategy also includes working with the website's blog. This should contain all sorts of information, starting with the latest updates and going further with informative articles about relevant issues. Lately, it has become popular to do AMAs (ask me anything). This helps investors' deal with any questions they may come up with.

Post-ICO Management And Product Development

When an ICO has been concluded successfully, the funds are collected as expected. It is time to use them for further product development, as stated in the company's white paper. At the next stage, it is necessary to run product tryouts and make improvements where needed. Every company has an individual roadmap within their ICO development plan, and all milestones should be followed, providing explanations and information on progress to the community.

In conclusion, there is an intense market pressure for non-blockchain products and companies when it comes to raising moneg through ICOs. No doubt, it is much better than the alternatives, and you won't even have to give up board seats. Unless governments come up with some heavy handed legal measures, ICOs will inevitably become the go-to way to raise money in the near future.

You have a non-blockchain company and wish to jump on the bandwagon? I urge you to go ahead and not limit yourself because of soon-to-be outdated opinions. Just make sure you avoid the securities pitfalls and be creative with the token and the benefits buyers are given (beyond price speculation) - there's absolutely nothing wrong with raising money though an ICO, even if you're not a blockchain company!

Blockchain today is much like the internet in 1997: It's only the beginning of the boom. Five years from now we'll be looking back and laughing at how primitive ICOs were in 2018.Here our main topic of discussion started from the introduction of MVP and proceeded to stating reasons why MVP is needed and how to build an MVP. Few examples of MVP were incorporated to lead us straight into the unusual truth about why an MVP alone won't make you successful. Lack of flexibility along with Post-ICO development period were discussed to drive the chapter towards the conclusion which included using tokens, developing the product and Post-ICO management and Product Development phase.

Chapter 9
Rules & Regulations

The elephant in the room, when it comes to ICO is no doubt regulation. In fact, many don't realize the important of understanding in complete depth everything there is to know about rules and regulations of this new form of fundraising. In retrospect, there are three types of regulatory regimes that we see around the world:

- Outright hostility (China)
- Cautious and strict, but still open (USA)
- Open, friendly, and liberal (Switzerland)

The interesting thing about ICOs is that all business is conducted electronically on global blockchain networks. This makes it incredibly easy for companies to locate themselves where the ICO rules and regulations are the most appropriate.

What is the authority that regulates ICO? Every country has a different regulatory authority. For instance, the

United States Securities and Exchange Commission (SEC) takes charge of regulating financial markets in the U.S. Additionally, they also have jurisdiction over new ICOs when there are considered as investment products and sold to American consumers.

It is somewhat easy to create a legal ICO in the United States, even then the SEC follows a set of rules and regulations known as the Howey Test. It helps to determine if the ICO is a tradable security or not. What happens to the ICOs that fail the Howey Test? Such ICOs are subject to all the same regulations as public stocks, and they must be registered and duly follow strict securities law.

It is difficult to create a compliant and publicly-traded security due to financial and logistic burdens in place for most companies. Startups on the blockchain are very much in the same vein. Therefore, if you wish to launch an ICO that is available to American consumers, the ICO will have to pass the Hovey Test. Regulations put forward by the European Union also clearly mirror the guidelines given by the Howey Test.

Following are some of the best practices that can be used, taken from other crowdsales on how to create a compliant ICO.

Regulations Around Investment Vehicles And Securities

Regulators have begun to divert their attention toward cryptocurrencies, only after the recent boom happened in Ethereum-based ICOs. Securities commissions have been set up in order to protect consumers from dangerous or fraudulent investments that are also rampant.

Additionally, the recent increase in ICOs also means there is an increase in pump and dump schemes, where tokens that have no value are introduced in the market and then dumped. This is a huge issue for regulators, who are understandably concerned about fraudulent ICO activity. What problems are faced by regulators when it comes to regulating ICOs circulating in the market? In many cases, it is difficult to perform an audit of an ICO or to evaluate a token's legitimacy.

Keeping the above in mind, the SEC has issued certain guidelines to consumers who are thinking of investing in ICOs, but they haven't issued clear guidelines for the creators of ICO tokens regarding compliance. The only advice given is to consult a lawyer, which is important but not the only thing to consider. The SEC has resorted to sorting ICOs into two basic categories (in the absence of ICO-specific regulations and guidelines. The two categories are: security and not a security.

What are securities? They are publicly traded investment opportunities. In the United States, a security via an IPO (or initial public offering) of a corporation's stock can be created. Another way this can be done is via lighter-weight regulations known as Regulations D, S, A plus, or crowdfunding. Once registered with the SEC, a security will have to go through audits, anti-money laundering laws, and Know Your Customer rules… which complicates the process of creating and administering an ICO.

However, over the past year most ICOs have sought to avoid classification as a security to reduce regulatory issues. ICOs hoping to avoid regulatory hurdles often emphasize a token's utility that is being issued as a form of currency on a new software platform. By doing so, it is hoped that the token will be given a clear value, almost as if the consumer were purchasing a gift card or license to use the future platform.

Another option being taken by many ICOs to avoid securities regulation is to structure the ICO as a donation initiative to a not-for-profit organization. Contributions to the ICO are considered donations as a result, and not purchases of a tradeable security.

While both of these approaches may make sense for some ICOs, they're not foolproof to prevent security classification. This is where the Howey Test comes in the picture. The Howey Test provides a clearer outline for what constitutes a security.

Howey Test – What Is It?

We get the Howey Test from a 1946 United States Supreme Court case known to the world as SEC vs. Howey Co. In the case, the U.S. Supreme Court created a simple test to help determine if a transaction is considered an 'investment contract' or not. If determined effectively, the transaction is subject to securities law and regulations. This test is still taken as a standard by which the new financial instruments are judged in the United States, including today's ICOs.

How does the test work for ICOs? According to the Howey Test, a transaction is only considered an 'investment contract' if:

- Money is invested in a common enterprise or company
- Investor expects profit from the investment
- Profit comes from the efforts of someone other than the investor

In the case of ICOs, the second point is the most important. If you're promoting your ICO as a way to make money, then you are promoting a security, according to the SEC. If, on the other hand, you're promoting your new tokens as a pre-order of a future product with no future return on investment, then you're likely in the clear with regulatory compliance.

However, according to Andrew Chapin who spoke with the SEC about his ICO, while the Howey Test forms the foundation for the SEC's classification of ICOs, the SEC reserves the right to make judgment calls about new ICOs on a case by case basis.

Another Regulatory Option: Exclude U.S. Investors

It is always uncertain whether an ICO will pass the Howey Test or not. Rather dealing with this uncertainty, many new companies choose to forego U.S. investment altogether! The following piece of news will shock you – nearly every major token sale conducted in the past six months has excluded U.S. investors. This means if a U.S. citizen wants to purchase a token, they will have to wait until it is listed on public exchanges.

However there is an exception to this rule, which is that accredited investors in the United States. The SEC has certified these individuals to participate in speculative investments. Otherwise, strict KYC practices generally exclude American investors and keep new ICOs out of reach of the SEC.

The keys to creating a compliant ICO that follows the Howey Test are simple. First, make sure that token purchasers do not expect to profit, and say so publicly before the launch starts. Second, make it clear that your token has a specific purpose and utility. Buyers should know what they're getting in return for their purchase. Alternatively, you can forego the SEC entirely by excluding U.S. investors from your token sale.

ICO Regulations By Country

European Union – Allowed/Subject To Future Regulations

ICOs are allowed in the EU, although there are certain restrictions. They are only allowed, if give adherence to Anti-Money Laundering (AML) and Know Your Customer

(KYC) policies and the required business regulations and licenses. Keeping in mind ICOs business function.

On November 13, 2017, the European Securities and Market Authority took a stricter stance on ICOs, however, declaring that an ICO represents a high risk to investors and requiring firms dealing with ICOs to meet relevant regulatory requirements. This suggests that the EU is ready to embrace America's position on ICOs, which is a reversal of the Union's previous position.

United Kingdom – Allowed, But Subject To Future Regulations

The United Kingdom has, like most other nations issued investors warning regarding the unregulated nature of ICOs. Here the Financial Conduct Authority argues that there is still a very good probability and chance of losing an entire investment, even if the ICO is acting in good faith.

Typically, ICO projects which are in early stage of development and their business models are usually experimental. The United Kingdom perceives altcoins as 'private currency, similar to Disney Dollars at Disney properties. In the current, stratosphere, ICO operators are completely free to interpret existing laws and regulations as they see ideal for their own properties. What about ICO testing? Although, the UK is utilizing the 'regulatory sandbox' strategy to test ICOs and altcoins, new regulations are thought to be released soon. Additionally, a ban is in place currently when it comes to purchasing altcoins by several of the nation's banks.

United States – Allowed, But Heavily Regulated

ICO rules and regulations are different from state to state. Some states have no regulations at all in place, while others have regulations that require making deposits in equal to or in excess of all local regulations. Some states have regulations in place that require a license for business to engage in altcoin creation activities. However there aren't any current regulations that specifically ban ICOs, on the federal level. ICOs are required by law to be registered and licensed the same as if they weren't ICOs.

This also means registration must be done with the SEC if the ICO is set out to sell or trade securities. The SEC has found recently that some altcoins may be used as securities, therefore opening the possibility to SECs ruling in the future. However some commissioners think that most ICOs are securities and should therefore be treated as such. Additionally, ICOs in the United States are expected to adhere to the practices laid down by AML/KYC. If failing to do so, can leave an ICO open to legal action and even possible seizure.

The United States has also moved to recognize celebrity endorsements of ICOs to be illegal unless all compensation involved is disclosed.

India – Allowed, BUT Heavily Regulated

There is a ban on purchasing altcoin, led by several of the nation's credit card processors and major bangs throughout India. Additionally, altcoin purchase and usage is heavily discouraged by the government. In fact, the Reserve Bank of India has banned altcoin usage in the banking system.

Australia – Allowed/Regulated

Australia was one of the first countries to formally launch ICO rules and regulations. The country requires ICOs to comply and adhere to the Corporations Act, those ICOs that involve combined investment. This is wanted so that those shares can be tracked, if the ICO shares. It is also important because disclosure documents can be issued and financial services license can be issued if the ICO offers financial advice to its customers.

However, Australia has issued draft laws that would allow the establishment of a regulatory sandbox for FinTech startups that would allow them to operate without being fully licensed.

China - Banned

ICOs are banned for all businesses and individuals by order of the People's Bank of China. Chinese ICOs that have completed their funding cycles have been requested to refund any altcoins raised.

The PBoC has indicated it will investigate any company or individual found to be in violation of its ruling. The trading of altcoins is also being targeted. Officially, individuals are still allowed to hold altcoins.

In Conclusion

The world's attitude towards ICOs is slowly changing and shifting, as a result of rules and regulations in place by the concerned authorities. The above-mentioned nations and major financial institutions have taken a strong stance on ICOs and altcoins – be it for the continuing international crackdown on fraudulent and malicious ICOs, a nationalistic cornering of the local altcoin market, or recognition of the inherent risk in the turbulent ICO space.

Oddly, however, there has been an embracing of distributed ledgers, the technology behind altcoins, even if much of the world has strong reservations about its public proof-of-concept. Many of the nations that have the strongest stance against altcoins are the most optimistic about integrating blockchain into their existing protocols. What is the takeaway for investors here?

Taking the temperature of the regulatory environment for ICOs is a wise course for any investor wading into the space. Understanding the ever-changing nature of regulation serves an investor well because keeping an eye on regulatory trends will enable investors to avoid running afoul of the legal requirements that come with investment.

It is the responsibility of the investor to do his or her due diligence before investing in any ICO. While regulations can help to reduce the investment risk, the best risk reduction practice is extensive research and preparation.

In this particular chapter, we shed light on the rules and regulations which are mandatory to be followed and abide by. The initial topic was of regulations around investment vehicles and securities along with explanation regarding Howey Test can be beneficial in letting you move forward. The final factor consisted of ICO regulations by country, describing the rules of first world major countries.

Chapter 10

Crowdfunding & Pitch

One thing that startups are always looking for when starting their ICO project is investors and a lot of funding to jumpstart that particular project. This is where crowdfunding comes in the picture. It is an incredible way for people, businesses and charities to raise money. The concept is that… crowdfunding prompts individuals or organizations to become investors (or donate to) crowdfunding projects implemented by another company or startup, in return for a potential profit or reward.

How Does Crowdfunding Work

Suppose your company wants to raise money to work on and jumpstart a particular ICO project… the aid and assistance of crowdfunding can be taken. Money can be effectively raised through crowdfunding. Although, the startup will need to pitch or sell the idea to investors before any success can be made in investing for the project. This can be done by posting details of the project, business or idea on a crowdfunding website or platform. What does this mean for the startup? The business can avoid going to the bank, and collect funds from the people or organizations that have the ability or interest to invest.

Suppose you are interested in crowdfunding for an ICO project but you have no idea what to do first or how to relay your idea to interested investors. The best thing to do is pitch the idea. Visit any crowdfunding website and you should be able to see an overview of the projects that are pitched on the platform at a regular basis. Investors interested in investing will be registered on the website, to see the pitches and find out more details about a project. Only then will the individual or organization decide to invest in the project.

Here is the thing to remember: some crowdfunding websites charge investors a fee, which may be a percentage of any profit they make. This is one reason why individuals and organizations will go through the details of any project with a comb, getting right into the deeper end of the project. Investors look for more details regarding a project they are interested in, so what are the project details you might want to focus on?

- How much you want to raise
- How much you have raised so far
- How much is the share in the business offered (if relevant)
- What the money will be used for
- How long is the pitch open for
- How many people have already invested
- When will investors receive in return for investing (i.e. shares in the company)

An important note to consider is, the investment can only go ahead if the startup or business raises the full amount. Usually, investors are given a 14-day 'cooling-off' period in case their mind changes.

Different Types Of Crowdfunding

There are several types of crowdfunding. The most common ones are:

Investment-Based Crowdfunding

In this type of crowdfunding, individuals and organizations invest in a business and receive a stake in return. The stake in return are normally shares.

Loan-Based Crowdfunding

In this type of funding, individuals or companies lend money to the startup in return for a set interest rate. This type of crowdfunding is also called peer-to-peer or peer-to-business lending.

Donation-Based Crowdfunding

In this type of funding, the startup donates to a person or charity. They may also be promised something in return.

Reward-Based Crowdfunding

In this type of crowdfunding, you give money in return for a reward which is linked to the project or a cause that the startup is supporting.

Are the above crowdfunding types regulated in anyway? Neither donation nor reward-based crowdfunding are regulated by the Financial Conduct Authority, but loan and investment-based crowdfunding are.

Benefits Of Crowdfunding

Though funding is most always the main goal of a crowdfunding campaign, it can also become an incredible way to gain visibility, validate businesses, and grow an investor's customer base.

Following are some common benefits of crowdfunding that are enjoyed by all the parties involved in the process.

More Efficient Than Traditional Fundraising

It can be difficult to pay attention or give the necessary time that is needed to pursue traditional financing demands, especially when a company is at the early-stage and focused on building and attracting seed capital. It makes a lot of sense to seek out other means of collecting funds, such as setting up a crowdfunding campaign on the appropriate platform. In fact compared to applying for a loan or seeking out accredited investors yourself, crowdfunding is a far more effective and efficient way to attract the right investors towards your ICO project.

All you need is the right crowdfunding platform for this purpose, which will help tell your business's story, produce a quick video, set up some enticing rewards, and benefit from having everything in one centralized location – at a place where potential investors can easily find your ICO project and business.

Place To Build Traction, Social Proof, And Validation

One thing that will chart the way forward for your company or startup is validation and social proof. This can only be had effectively with the help of a strong and highly visible crowdfunding campaign. What happens when potentials show interest in your startup's product or service? This will generate social proof – i.e. demonstrating to potential investors that other people do believe in what you are doing. This will prompt early adopters to vet for and buy into your idea, causing others to follow suit.

In turn, social proof is automatically translated into traction (whether it's a large number of backers, pre-orders, or media attention) that is an invaluable thing as you pitch the idea to other investors.

Therefore, crowdsourcing has grown into an excellent way for entrepreneurs and early-stage companies for the above reasons and benefits. In conclusion, some of the most powerful ways a crowdfunding campaign can help build more startup momentum (as compared than other financing methods) are:

- More efficient than traditional fundraising
- Generates traction, social proof, and validation
- An opportunity for crowdsourced brainstorming to refine your idea
- Gains you early adopters and loyal advocates
- Doubles as marketing and media exposure

How can you ensure potential investors are attracted to your idea and even subscribe to it? Designing a persuasive ICO pitch addressing investor concerns and considerations is the key to successfully selling your token. However, most startups spend too much time with an expert technical building the perfect block-chain based technology, not paying attention to how they will jumpstart the project.

They don't pay heed when it comes to developing and presenting a compelling ICO pitch to raise funds.

Following are some essential components that make up the general structure of a successful ICO pitch:

Prove You Are Solving A Real Problem By Leveraging Blockchain

So many ICO projects are introduced every year, where people don't really pay attention to the application of blockchain technology. In such occasions, this appears more to be an afterthought and potentially unnecessary. It is incumbent to know realize why you are building the blockchain application in the first place. It is also equally important to illustrate the complete magnitude of the problem you are hoping the application will solve. This will help more than anything else to get initial buy-in from investors.

The fact of the matter is that ICOs have gotten a bad rep because many people still believe ICO projects are mainly cash-grab opportunities for startups. Think about it: If the identified problem given to potential investors can be easily solved by using a database instead of your solution, why would anyone bother investing in the first place?

So, what should you keep in mind when creating a pitch for your ICO project? Ideally, it should be made clear that your solution provides relevancy to the problem at hand, which people are facing at this current moment. Never pick a problem that people theorize might happen, even in the near future.

Sound Token Economics

Many crypto-investors are usually interested in one thing – value appreciation of the tokens they purchase. Investors can also have doubts of a dud token investment, which can be allayed by blochchain founders by clearly showcasing how their tokens are created, how they will be used and why the tokens will grow in value over-time.

Additionally, blockchain companies running ICOs mostly create utility tokens that can be spent or exchanged easily for services, rebates or goods. In this way, tokens get burnt after usage and become even scarcer. What is the result? The worth of the token increases naturally.

It is a good idea to make a case for your token's increasing value. This can be done by illustrating what the currency's circulation will look like as well as highlighting various scenarios for increasing demand, adoption and scarcity. Another tip to sway investors to your side is to communicate how the tokens will work in the grand scheme of the world.

Highlight Your Team's Competence

The thing about any company or solution is that it is the people and teams behind one project, who are responsible for making or breaking it. Ask yourself these questions:

- What are the technical strengths of the team?
- Do the members have any notable achievements or associations?

- Are their experiences relevant to the blockchain solution that is being offered?

Ideally, token holders and crypto-investors need to know the technology's longevity but additionally, they also want to find out the credentials of the people behind the project. This is why the first step to take is to identify some greatest strengths within the team. Another tip is to keep the format of the team profiles consistent.

An important tip to note and implement is the avoidance of general statements like: 'creator of multiple successful startups' which feature a boastful stance. What you can do instead is to always use quantitative numbers or facts to substantiate any such statements.

Write Your 'Post-ICO' Plan In Detail

There are some investors who buy tokens to HODL for the long-haul, meaning they don't sell them immediately after the ICO is over. This is done because they anticipate growth in value of the token. As such, they will want to know exactly what the founders plan to do in the months or years ahead. This is what is called a roadmap and it should include:

Marketing And Growth Plans

The community members willing to invest in the ICO project will want to know how acquisition and retaining will continue of new token holders. This is necessary as it will help instill confidence in token holders regarding the tokens and their affinity to staying relevant and valuable for a long time.

Project Timeline

It is an important requisite to have clear dates setup as doing so will help keep founders of the project accountable regarding their promises. Investors can also easily and closely track any progress of solution development. Implementing a simple linear illustrations usually works the best in these kinds of cases.

Financial Plan And ICO Proceeds

This is one of the most important piece of information for any token investor i.e. the mechanics of the raise and how the ICO proceeds will be distributed. Companies or individuals thinking of investing in a particular ICO project will need to know the various factors, which will be considered in their purchase.

The different factors that are commonly considered before making an investment are:

- Hard caps and limits
- Number of tokens
- Token distribution methods

However, (perhaps unfortunately) there have been many blockchain companies that have taken token holders for a ride. They are known to misspend proceeds or never get any closer to realizing their base solution idea.

Additionally, investors interested in ICO have even become increasingly wary of projects with incredibly high token caps. Therefore, it is a good idea to only raise money that is needed, which is an important thing to consider when pitching your ICO crowdfunding idea.

An example of a success token sale and how proceeds are to be raised during an ICO is conducting a transparent breakdown. It is inherently difficult to navigate in the new world of cryptocurrency and blockchain, especially when efforts are also being made to gain traction in the initial stages.

However, as with any difficult endeavor, strategies that work will leave patterns and we can learn from these successes and apply the lessons to our own projects.

How To Engage With Potential Investors

Startups need to find some common ground with their potential investors before engaging with them. This is true even before the upcoming launch of your ICO or token.

Over here, I am not talking about the global community of crypto investors but about the pre-token/ICO raise.

There are some steps that need to be taken, things that must be done for this to come to light. There are also some things that must not be done.

Please Don't

- Never ever send a generic email to potential investors – it is obvious and likely to be deleted without a glance
- Don't be over-confident – in the end, there is a fine line between confidence and arrogance

Please Do

Do your homework. This cannot be reiterated enough! Ensure to conduct a thorough research, covering all the areas that you would need to work on. Answer the following questions:

- Why should a particular investor give you their hard-earned money?
- What is your connection with the investor?
- Do you have anything common with the investor?

All of this information can be easily found with just a few clicks on LinkedIn,

Other considerations to think about when designing your ICO pitch is paying attention to how an investor thinks. As it is, his or her logic to invest in a particular project will be pretty simple:

- How will this project increase my status, my value and my wealth?
- Is the team experienced enough to help me in achieving my goals?
- Does this team know how to deal with money?
- If I invest, how do I know these guys won't lose the money?

In a nutshell, all the above points and questions cover everything that any investor is thinking about. So, this is what you should and shouldn't if you want to be heard and chosen by potential investors.

Important Considerations

- **Don't** – write a lengthy introduction about a happy and prosperous blockchain future for the world and its inhabitants, as far as the digital economics is concerned. Everyone who has ever invested in ICO knows this a general and often unclear statement.

- **Do** – go straight to the point when presenting your ICO pitch! Discuss in concise points what the project is about, what solution the project aims to fix, and how it will work. Also, how you plan to execute the mechanics of the project should also be discussed.

- **Don't** – repeat content taken straight from the ICO website. Why? This particular resource is open for everybody, so the investors will most likely know what is already on the website. Additionally, this resource often contains too much insignificant information.

- **Do** – show and tell something (anything relevant) that the audience and potential investors won't get or find anywhere else i.e. public sources. Show and tell something that is relevant to the central questions mentioned above.

- **Don't** – show screenshots with your team (taken from the website again), especially if there isn't a celebrity or lead around there. Think about it, nobody knows your colleagues. Nobody needs to remember or even see their names and faces for them to want to invest.

- **Do** – speak like the ICO pro you are! What topics to talk about? For starters, how you plan to use somebody's money when an investor invests. You will have to tell how the projects will attract and bring profits eventually. So, show your awareness by giving a short but insightful speech. Remember to keep it SHORT and INSIGHTFUL!

So if you do, six or even three minutes will be enough for you. The elevator speech is essentially more shortly —

just 30 seconds! No one complains. Conversely, people are trying to develop the short-speech skills hardly. So you should do the same.

The key to a good pitch is telling the investors a story. Create a setup with the characters and the background, provide them with a conflict and give them your ICO as a solution. Make sure that you highlight the benefits, and the features of the project. To conclude, your pitch shouldn't be too complicated to understand. The story has to be emotional in order to be remember-able.

What about crowdfunding woes? Complete your due diligence the same way you would with a casual startup equity investment. But rather than have your legal team investigate, look at what's available regarding the ICO's white paper, website details, founding team etc. Providing assurance to your investors is most important here. While having in-depth technical knowledge isn't mandatory for the current crowdfunding model, ICO makes it inevitable.

In this chapter we discussed how crowdfunding works along with different types of crowdfunding does. The main focus was on the benefits of crowdfunding, leading to other factors being discussed as well. The conclusive phase incorporated the steps on how to engage with potential investors and few important considerations before the concluding chapter.

Chapter 11

Launch

Have you noticed how people are attracted to a new thing or technology due to a certain quality, until slowly but surely that thing or technology becomes widely popular and ever-growing? The same thing can be said of cryptocurrencies and the blockchain technology. The exponential increase in market cap indicates that more and more people are learning about cryptocurrencies and considering buying some of them. In fact, this growing popularity of cryptocurrencies has incentivized many businesses to look into this technology and take advantage of the growing popularity as well as the numerous possibilities offered by these technologies.

One thing to remember when thinking of investing or even using it as a crowdfunding opportunity is that while the blockchain technology and cryptocurrencies are certainly not perfect, making far worldwide adoption impossible – there have been some use cases where adoption of this technology has shown to be superior compared to traditional counterparts.

What are the main reasons traditional crowdfunding platforms are a thing of the past? Traditional crowdfunding platforms often take a relatively large fee for using their platform (sometimes up to 30%). Additionally, these solutions are often heavily regulated. On the other hand, ICOs provide businesses with complete ownership of their crowdfunding campaigns and since ICOs don't require a special platform to be used, there aren't any fees that need to be paid to begin.

However, launching an ICO isn't a walk in the park. In addition to traditional operations associated with launching a crowdfunding campaign, creating an ICO requires some additional know-how and operations for a successful launch.

Launching An ICO Campaign

If you have come this far in the book, chances are that you are considering launching an ICO campaign and reaping the benefits. There are many examples of campaigns that were started by individuals and companies, such as the Useless Ethereum Token, which was very likely created by a single person (in no time at all) and still managed to raise almost $200,000 in contributions. Similarly, your future project will need quite a significant amount of time as well as a dedicated team to attract substantial funds to jumpstart the ICO project.

Just A Small Disclaimer Before Proceeding

it is rather expensive to host a successful ICO from scratch. It takes approximately $60,000 to launch a campaign, but then again the final number can depend on the project and decided goals. Another thing, launching an ICO campaign is a time-consuming process. In many cases, pre-public engagement phase (which considers all the processes before the first big announcement is made) takes six months to one year, which is a rough estimate.

Are you serious about launching an ICO? To make the launch easier, following are some important aspects that must be considered by businesses before jumping on the ICO train.

Do You Even Need To Launch An ICO

First things first, do you need to launch an ICO project to raise funds? There should always be a true use case behind the urge to create your own cryptocurrency. What does it mean? You must have a solution that really works from the problem faced by the targeted audience and potential investors. A solution that is only relevant for that particular problem. What will happen if you create your own currency with the intention of raising funds with the ICO? The coin's value will drop after the ICO is launched, as there won't be anything to keep the coin's price at a certain level. This means there won't be many people interested in buying your coin.

It is a better idea to not even create a coin in the first place if there will be difficulties in integrating the cryptocurrency to your business. The reasons are simple – launching an ICO requires plenty of extra work and creates additional obligations to your team. So, without having a real use case and lack of supporters, the effort isn't worth it.

Gather Your Team

It is time to choose and create your team members after you successfully establish the need of an ICO and a problem that requires that solution. Having a capable team behind the scenes and at your help will take your vision from just an idea to reality! Also, it is better to realize that achieving your idea on your own will be a lot more difficult than taking the help of a dedicated and professional team.

Ensure that all aspects of your company are covered when gathering the team for this project. In addition to traditional skills like marketing, finances, and product or service development – launching an ICO also requires people who are able to deal with cryptocurrencies and ICOs. What are the requirements of enlisted team members? Your team has to be professional and well-versed when it comes to establishing goals. They also have to ensure whether the project is feasible or not, and guide you accordingly. The team must also be able to deliver all made promises.

Another thing, even though cryptocurrencies are mostly associated with anonymity, launching such a project doesn't coincide well with keeping identities secret. People who are interested in investing in your project will want to know just who is working on it.

Analyze And Write Down Your Plan

It is a good idea to write down exactly what, why, and how you are planning to create the product or service. Of course, this is usually done when you have your idea and team. What is the base of a successful project? Creating a detailed action plan with defined tasks that are assigned to the respective people, along with specific deadlines.

When the plan is completed, everyone in your team knows exactly what their job is, what needs to be done and when it has to be completed, and this plan should be converted into a whitepaper and a roadmap. The whitepaper lends valuable assistance when it comes to acting as a complete guide for your business and its product/service. Make sure to include the company's structure, specifics of the product as well as how you plan on creating it in the first place.

Other important details relevant to the project and what investors want to know are also included in the whitepaper.

Create The Cryptocurrency And ICO Structure

This is the easiest part of the entire process. There are many different platforms that provide businesses with the opportunity to easily create their own currency. All you have to do is give a small fee, which will help create the coin in minutes!

Some of the most popular platforms that can be used for this purpose are:

- Ethereum

- Waves
- NXT
- Bitshares
- NEM

These platforms offer thorough guides on how to create your coin, so it shouldn't be above anyone's ability, especially for someone who is creating their own company.

Marketing And Communication

Both are essential aspects that need to be considered before launching your ICO. What will you do about promoting and letting the world hear about your project and ICO? One of the major things that can be done is to create a webpage that includes all the necessary information, your whitepaper, and roadmap etc. Ideally, a countdown till the beginning as well as an order form after the launch (to make purchase easy) should also be included.

Additionally, the website should include some explainer videos, photos of the team and anything else that will help create extra clarity and trust in investors.

The next step is to use marketing tactics and tips to help spread the word. You must also communicate and interact with your bankers and investors, keeping them in the loop on every development and keeping them up to date with the latest news and progress.

Delivery Of Promises

And finally, before you celebrate your successful campaign, you have to make sure that the life of your company doesn't end with the end of the ICO. Now you have a lot of people who have purchased your coins in the hopes that you create your product/service, solve their problems and actually deliver on your promises. Don't let these people down!

It is optimal to launch an ICO with at least an alpha version of a product, and even better, a beta version—and when it comes to soft caps and hard caps, or the advertised lower and upper limits for an ICOs' fundraising activity, it is important to keep the figures realistic.

BLOCKCHAIN SECRETS

To summarize what we have covered so far in the book, ICO stands for initial coin offering. It refers to the unregulated raising of funds for cryptocurrency venture. The first ICO was founded by J.R. Willett in 2013 but it was not until 2014, during the launch of Ethereum that we saw a boom in funding. ICOs are important because they are useful for the growth of small businesses.

Coins are used for the transfer of money whereas, tokens can be used to transfer ownership of almost everything. Tokens can be used in business for digital objects, cryptocurrency, verifiable voting etc. Some of the most common reasons why an ICO fails are lack of communication, low security, no PR or marketing etc. An IPO is the distribution of shares and other investments. Ideally, an IPO works well under a centralized corporation.

Like any business, your Blockchain business needs well-defined goals, ideas, and objectives. ICO to be considered one part of the Blockchain Business, but not the only goal. This is the mistake most businesses are making that they make the ICO the only goal for their blockchain business to be successful. This book is designed to make you successful in the ICO, but it doesn't mean that this should be your only or sole purpose for the business.

We also discussed the importance of ICO whitepapers and how to write one. Whitepaper and roadmaps are usually used to define these aspects. Whitepaper describes the ICO in detail. It focuses on the problem that will be solved. It lists the goals, objectives, and future plans. The roadmap describes the timeline of your ICO. It explains each stage of the project from its initial phase.

A whitepaper is an in-depth report about a specific topic. The following aspects are needed to create an attractive whitepaper for any ICO:

- Promoter's location
- Problem and its solution
- Token's description
- Blockchain
- Qualification of your team
- The risks

Having a good website up and running prior to launching the ICO project was also discussed. A website can provide potential investors with sufficient information about the

Blockchain and token. It can effectively portray the team and the project. Once the website is created, make sure it does not crash. Make it easy to navigate and understand. Make sure it is available on each technological device. The chapter further explores the things that you should avoid while building an ICO website.

These days, announcing your ICO is not enough, you have to go an extra mile to receive substantial investment. These marketing tactics will create a buzz for your ICO to attract more investors. You can use the available platforms to raise awareness of your ICO such as bitcointalk. Reddit and social media are the ideal platforms to market your ICO. Comparatively, Twitter has a larger crypto community. Furthermore, marketing on ICO-specific sites will boost chances for investments.

For most of the time, investors are not concerned about the projects behind the ICO. They are more focused on the flip tokens. Using PR for your ICO will be the most effective aspect.

The team behind your ICO project can be a vital determinant of the investment. Make sure you have the right members in your team. Consider their qualification and ability to complete the assigned task. An investor might refuse to invest in your project if there is an ineffective team. A great ICO is evaluated on the basis of the following:

- Search on social media
- Googling photos
- Connecting to the team
- Size of the team
- Level of team cooperation
- Are there any experts on a specific area?
- The insignificance of advisors
- Crypto industry experience
- Is there an international team?

We also discussed the need for an MVP in launching an ICO campaign.

Let me explain by saying that you don't need an MVP to be successful in ICO. But I have seen on numerous occasions where MVP was available and made a huge difference when the investors could see the demo of the product during roadshows.

A minimum viable product (MVP) is a developmental technique where we build a prototype of Product behind the ICO. This doesn't mean that your product has to be perfect but there has to be something. We repeatedly test the product before moving for the launch. Taking the customers feedback to improve the product can be vital for the final version of the ICO.

One reason why people prefer ICO and blockchain technology is the lax in regulations. Sure the concerned authorities do provide a set of guidelines and regulations but compared to traditional crowdfunding methods, this one's still better.

In the United States, the SEC is used to set the rules and regulations for ICO. Passing the Howey test can be pivotal. In Europe, the ESMA is considered to be friendlier than SEC. In Australia, the ASIC has provided guidelines for ICO. China had placed a ban on ICO, which was not effective. However, it has introduced a new set of rules and regulations, which suggests that China will lift the ban. On the other hand, there are no official guidelines for ICO in India.

What is crowdfunding? Crowdfunding refers to the act of raising funds for a project or venture from a large number of people. To proficiently pitch your ICO project, you need to engage the investors, so:

- Conduct research on the investor
- Find a connection between you and the investor
- Communicate important information about how you will resolve a problem

There are certain things that you should avoid during the pitch.

- Try not to send out a general email
- Do not be presumptuous
- Do not be too confident. It might be mistaken for arrogance.

How well you launch your crowdfunding campaign depends on how many investors are attracted towards the project. In turn, this depends on how well your sales pitch is for the project. The key to a good pitch is telling the investors a story. Create a setup with the characters and the background, provide them with a conflict and give them your ICO as a solution. Make sure that you highlight the benefits, and the features. In conclusion, your pitch shouldn't be too complicated to understand. The story has to be emotional in order to be remember-able.

Lastly and most importantly, we discussed different aspects in earlier chapters that need to be considered before launching the ICO campaign, and they are as follow:

Before launching your ICO, consider the following aspects:

- Think whether you need to launch the ICO.
- Gather the team.
- Write the launch plan.
- Create the structure for the ICO.
- Start the marketing campaign.
- Launch the product.

Future Of ICO

There is no doubt that the ICO market has seen a lot of success. Additionally, there are some of the most fundamentally strong projects launched in the market, but a correction is due in time. A lack of regulation was and had always been one of the key factors that fueled the ICO buying frenzy, but that is slowly changing as discussed in the previous chapter.

So, we could expect some red-taping soon around ICOs in the coming years! As well as implementation of a strict framework, which isn't necessarily bad news as it will help in separation of good projects from the bad ones and potential ICO scams. For a regular investor, it is important to weigh the benefits, risks and potential legal upswings of the ICO landscape before investing.

BLOCKCHAIN SECRETS

if you like us to help with you your Blockchain Project, feel free to reach out to our team at support@jagjassel.com

Thank you!

Jag Jassel

JAG JASSEL

www.ingramcontent.com/pod-product-compliance
Lightning Source LLC
Chambersburg PA
CBHW031618210526
45464CB00004B/1632